AMERICAN RESISTANCE

Surveying the crowd at the 2019 Women's March in Washington, DC.

AMERICAN RESISTANCE

From the Women's March to the
Blue Wave

DANA R. FISHER

Columbia University Press
New York

Columbia University Press
Publishers Since 1893
New York   Chichester, West Sussex
cup.columbia.edu
Copyright © 2019 Dana R. Fisher
All rights reserved

A complete cataloging-in-publication record
is available from the Library of Congress.
ISBN 978-0-231-18764-0 (cloth : alk. paper)
ISBN 978-0-231-54739-0 (e-book)
LCCN 2019018989

Columbia University Press books are printed
on permanent and durable acid-free paper.
Printed in the United States of America

Cover design: Noah Arlow

CONTENTS

PREFACE

MY MOM died on the day of the 2018 midterm elections after an agonizing battle with dementia. After voting with my kids in the morning, we were waiting for the returns to begin coming in when I got the call from the hospice nurse. Although my mom wasn't particularly civically engaged, she was an outspoken progressive who voted regularly, kept up with national politics, and adored Rachel Maddow. My mom had not paid much attention to my work on this book, although she had read my previous books, underlining as she made her way through them. In one of our last real conversations in early fall of 2018, she made it very clear that she thought the title "American Resistance" was a stinker.

Before the dementia had overtaken her, my mom would tell people that her greatest success was that she had raised three strong-willed and independent daughters in a changing world.

Coming of age in the 1950s, she grew up during the era when being a woman in America changed substantially: she was neither old enough to be comfortable following through with traditional expectations, nor young enough to feel comfortable marching in the streets and burning her bras.

Even as she tried to find a path that made her feel fulfilled, she infused my sisters and me with an understanding that being a woman in the United States required that we create our own identities, speak up for ourselves, and pay attention. Thanks to these efforts by my mom, my sisters and I have all created lives that involve clear professional identities that are interwoven with full personal lives that include families. As every working woman with children will tell you, every day is a challenge. But I believe it is one that we were more prepared for thanks to my mom.

Although my sisters and I took different paths, we all fit the profile of the majority of the participants in the Resistance: highly educated, white women, with varying levels of civic engagement and political experiences. At the same time, our participation in the Resistance (and the ways my sisters and I have gotten involved and stayed involved over the past two years) varies substantially in what we each have done and where and how we have focused our efforts.

On November 6, 2018, the people of the United States elected a diverse class of legislators into the House of Representatives, a group that included more women and more people of color than ever before. The outcome of the election would have made my mom happy. At the same time, the 2018 election was plagued with allegations of electoral inequities around the country that were linked to voter suppression and gerrymandering. Clearly, there is still much more work to be done.

This book began as a side project that took advantage of the fact that I had a lot of experience surveying at large-scale demonstrations and a big protest was coming to Washington, D.C.—the January 2017 Women's March. My colleagues and I put together our survey specifically to see how many of the different factions of the progressive movement made it into the streets for the Women's March, but as the Resistance grew the project expanded along with it.

In many ways, studying the American Resistance over these past two years has been therapeutic. It has also reinforced my belief in the need for strong social science research, which is the reason I left politics in the first place. Although there are numerous indicators of growing problems in our country, the *American Resistance* documents how many Americans woke up after the 2016 election, and it has reminded me of the beauty and resilience of our unique (and flawed) version of democracy.

This book is the product of hundreds of hours of observation in the streets of Washington, D.C. as hundreds of thousands of people marched again and again. It includes meetings with civic leaders and activists and numerous conversations with representatives of national progressive groups that were working to cultivate and channel this diverse and unwieldy movement. It tells the story of American democracy as it works to better itself and reminds us all that democracy is a work in progress; it is only as good as the people who take the time and energy to participate in it.

ACKNOWLEDGMENTS

IN CONTRAST to my previous big projects that turned into books, this project had a very different origin story: it began as a small collaborative project with colleagues at the University of Maryland after the 2016 election. I would like to thank Dawn Dow and Rashawn Ray for being interested in learning from the people who are participating in demonstrations—and for working with me to update my survey instrument and going out into the streets of Washington, D.C. with me on a number of occasions to collect data from protesters.

Although the project was initially unfunded, after our research during the 2017 Women's March earned so much media attention, the College for Behavioral and Social Sciences at the University of Maryland helped us raise the funds to purchase the electronic tablets that have been invaluable tools for data collection over the course of this project. It is possible to do this research without the tablets, but they make it possible to report findings based on the data we collect in almost real time. As a result, I have been able to analyze preliminary findings quickly and get the research out to a broader audience through the media.

I want to thank the many leaders of resistance groups who gave their time generously to speak with me while they were working tirelessly on the 2018 elections. This project also benefited from conversations with a number of scholars who have been invaluable sounding boards for my ideas. Michael Heaney and Lara Putnam talked with me on many occasions along the way, providing alternative perspectives from their own related research. As Sidney Tarrow was completing his own volume on the subject, he shared his insights and advice and even provided invaluable line edits to the drafts of every chapter. Lorien Jasny has been a wonderful collaborator who has worked with me to analyze some of the data in innovative ways and write up the findings for peer reviewed journals.

I also want to thank my editor, Eric Schwartz, who saw the potential of this project from the beginning and pushed me to write the book in a public way. The book is better thanks to his input and the great work of his colleagues at Columbia University Press. I also want to thank the Lund Centre for Sustainability for providing a brief home in exile as I worked on early drafts of this book in the fall of 2017.

In addition, I must show my gratitude to all the people who helped collect data out in the streets over these many months of resistance: Tuesday Barnes, Melissa Brown, Emily Campbell, Angel Eli Canales, Daniel Chen, Andrew Cheon, Jonathan Cox, Amanda Dewey, Dawn Dow, Scott Frickel, Genesis Fuentes,

ACKNOWLEDGMENTS

Shaun Genter, Hsiang-Yuan Ho, Han Kleman, Holly Koogler, Danielle Koonce, Angie O'Brien, Heather Randell, Rashawn Ray, Anya Galli Robertson, Nancy Sonti, Jade Weisletten, Cynthia Williams, Bill Yagatich, and Katatrina Yang, as well as the students of my activism and global movements class who discussed the project with me throughout the fall of 2018.

Finally, thanks to my sisters—my best friends—who remind me what family is meant to be. I must also give extra thanks to the little FishPatty clan, who spent the past twenty-eight months with my being frequently distracted or downtown surveying protesters. I'm sure my children have become desensitized to talk of progressive politics and the Resistance over meals. Once again, Aaron, you continue to be the best of partners and the best of friends.

AMERICAN RESISTANCE

Chapter One

HOW DID WE GET HERE?

IN SEPTEMBER of 2018, former president Barack Obama addressed a crowd at the University of Illinois at Urbana-Champaign. After months of living outside the political limelight and taking time off to be with his family and to kite surf with Richard Branson, the former president reentered public life before the midterm elections. Standing at the podium dressed in black and with a bit more gray around his ears, Obama announced:

> I'm here today because this is one of those pivotal moments when every one of us, as citizens of the United States, need[s] to determine just who it is that we are, just what it is that we stand for. And as a fellow citizen, not as an ex-president, but as a fellow citizen, I am here to deliver a simple message, and that is that you need to vote because our democracy depends on it. . . . The best way to protest is to vote.[1]

Although eloquently delivered, the former president's words were not particularly unique. A month later, during a conversation with Victoria Kaplan, the organizing director at MoveOn, I heard about all the ways her group was working to channel the outrage of the people marching in the streets into political action around the midterm elections. She expanded on Obama's address without even realizing it: "You can't just march and think that things are going to change. We march and we organize, *and* we vote."[2]

On the Saturday before the 2018 election, my older sister Lauren and I followed this advice and joined the effort to help get out the vote in Virginia's tenth district. We signed up through "The Last Weekend," a coalition of more than sixty groups that were working on the election.[3] Our assignment was to contact likely Democratic voters in a swing district that was about thirty minutes from each of our houses.

I had worked in politics and studied it since my graduation from college, so I am exactly the kind of person you might expect to see volunteering, but Lauren had traveled a different path. Working her way up from practicing law at a firm to serving as general counsel for a media company, Lauren had found little time for marches or political events beyond voting. Despite our varied political experiences, we both felt that we needed to do more than just vote in this midterm election. We arrived for our morning shift at a large house in Virginia in the suburbs just outside of Washington, D.C. In a cavernous basement recreation room, we joined a crowd of more than sixty people—locals and others who had traveled from nearby Maryland, the District of Columbia, and other districts in Virginia. The people in our Saturday morning shift looked exactly like what my research had found to be the bulk of the American Resistance—mostly middle-aged white women with a few bright pink hats and pins that said "#resist" on them.[4]

We received a quick pep talk from former Virginia governor Terry McAuliffe, instructions from the candidate's campaign on how to remind inconsistent Democratic voters to vote on election day, and were sent on our way. As I walked out the door into the crisp autumn morning, I shook my head and thought about what I was doing. More than twelve years after writing a book about fund-raising canvassing on the Left, and twenty-eight years after I had first canvassed in college, I was on my way back out onto turf to knock on doors—this time for an electoral campaign.

As my sister and I walked from house to house in this suburban area, crunching on the fall leaves, we quickly discovered that we were not the first canvassers to knock on these doors. These people had talked to other volunteers numerous times before we showed up on that last weekend. Most of the people who answered their door were very friendly (albeit a bit exasperated to have more strangers come calling) and showed interest in the election. One woman told us that she was on her way to pick up her daughter at the University of Virginia to bring her back to vote, a number of naturalized citizens eagerly confirmed that everyone who could vote in their households would be going to the polls on Tuesday, and a woman whose door was still adorned with skeletons from Halloween enthusiastically told us that she would be voting. Before shutting her cobweb-covered door, she announced: The Democrats will "flatten Barbara Comstock" (the Republican incumbent).

When we returned from knocking on likely voters' doors, I was surprised to find a traffic jam on the narrow suburban street as volunteers from the first shift reported back and the second shift got ready to go out into the district. Except for a brief chat with the former governor before he addressed the group that morning, Lauren and I had completed our work without having had any personal conversations or learned a single name among the volunteers. Nevertheless, our efforts helped to get the job done: On the following Tuesday, Jennifer Wexton beat Barbara Comstock, earning 56 percent of the vote. Moreover, turnout during this midterm election was notable; more than one million more people voted than had voted in the 2014 Virginia midterm elections, and only about six hundred thousand fewer people had voted than had turned out for the 2016 presidential election.[5]

In an email sent by a campaign coordinator after the election, we were told that our staging location "knocked on at least 25,000 doors and made contact with over 10,000 voters over the last three weekends before the election alone." The email concluded by quoting another volunteer and pointed out: "democracy is not some work of art that upon completion we can sit back and admire; it's an imperfect machine that requires constant maintenance."[6] Due in part to efforts by these volunteers, Wexton joined the blue wave of Democratic women serving in the 116th Congress that began in January 2019.

This book tells the story of the American Resistance. It begins on the cold and crowded streets of Washington, D.C.

at the January 2017 Women's March—the day after Donald Trump's inauguration—and ends in the congressional districts and communities around the country with the 2018 midterm elections in November.

WHAT IS THE RESISTANCE?

Before we get started, it is important to provide a clear definition of the Resistance:

> The American Resistance is people working individually and through organizations to challenge the Trump Administration and its policies. The Resistance includes people working as individual citizens (and non-citizens), through their professions as lawyers, scientists, artists, or professional athletes. It also includes organizations that run the gamut in terms of their levels of professionalization. The violent fringe that stirred in response to White supremacist activities around the US—the Antifa—is also part of the Resistance to the degree that it is focusing specifically on targeting the Trump agenda. In contrast to other claims, anonymous people in the Trump Administration who have challenged President Trump as a person but support his broader policy agenda are *not* part of the Resistance.[7]

In many ways, the Resistance is a countermovement to the Trump regime (like the Tea Party was a countermovement to the Obama administration and its policies).[8] Because it is a countermovement with a common enemy, it is possible to bring diverse streams of progressive activism together even though they have historically competed for resources, energy, and attention.[9] As I document in this book, the Resistance represents a merging of movements working together to form the river of resistance we see today. It includes Black Lives Matter, Occupy Wall Street, and the women's, antigun violence, and climate movements, among others.

At the same time, the bonds among these movements and the organizations that coordinate them are fragile and create a potential challenge to the strength and durability of the Resistance.[10] When I was conducting research for this book, some of the cleavages had already begun to show.[11] To understand the emergence of the American Resistance, we need to look more broadly at the political context from which it emerged.

Since Donald Trump won the presidential election without winning the popular vote, there has been substantial and continuous protest against the administration's plans for the United States. Street demonstrations are the most visible form of opposition to the administration and its policies. Hundreds of thousands marched in pink pussyhats on the day after the inauguration; thousands stood in airports to show support for an America that is open to immigrants; tens of thousands of people marched (some sporting brain hats) to support science; and hundreds of thousands circled the White House to show concern for climate change and to oppose the new administration's undoing much of the previous administration's progress toward regulating greenhouse gases[12]—and that was just the first three months of the Trump administration. In the summer of 2017, protests erupted around the United States in response to a counterprotester being killed during a white supremacists' rally and the president's response to the violence in Charlottesville, Virginia. As Americans repeatedly experience moral outrage in reaction to the statements and actions of President Trump, protests have continued around the country, and the American Resistance grows.

The Resistance has also extended into congressional districts. Constituents flooded the town hall meetings of their elected officials to voice their concerns. Pressure from members of the Resistance has been credited as one of the reasons the Republican-led Congress failed to repeal the Affordable Care Act in the fall of 2017[13] and the administration halted its family separation policy in the summer of 2018.[14] It also contributed to the Democrats winning in local elections around the United States a year after the 2016 election in November 2017.[15] U.S. government workers themselves have also resisted, with some starting rogue social media accounts[16] and others working to ensure data preservation.[17]

In response to the president and his administration's policies, members of presidential advisory panels have resigned, with the entirety of the President's Committee on the Arts and Humanities quitting with an explicit message of resistance.[18] In August 2017, a U.S. State Department science envoy stepped down from his appointment. The first letters of the paragraphs in his public resignation letter were an acrostic spelling the word "IMPEACH."[19] In other words, the election of Donald Trump has been a shot in the arm of democracy in the United

States. People are no longer bowling alone;[20] they are marching, yelling, and working together.

Despite the merger of different strains of the progressive movement spanning issues of race, class, gender, and sexual orientation, little has been written about *how* the progressive movement came together to form the Resistance.[21] This book documents the American Resistance by focusing on three of its interrelated components: Resistance in the streets, how groups are organizing the Resistance in the districts, and how people who have marched in the streets have engaged in Resistance in the districts. It concludes with a discussion of what the Resistance means for democracy and politics in the United States as well as for the upcoming 2020 election.

The Resistance is America's response to an out-of-touch Democratic Party, a president who shows no interest in compromise, and the reach of conservative donors using dark money.

THE 3MS OF POLITICS IN AMERICA
AND THE 2016 ELECTION

After the unexpected outcome of the 2016 election, a majority of postmortem discussions focused on problems with the Electoral College, Russian interference with the election, and, of course, FBI director James Comey's investigation into Secretary Hillary Clinton's emails.[22] At the same time, there was discussion about what I have called the "three M's" of politics in America and how they contributed to the outcome of the 2016 election: (1) the Man, (2) the Message, and (3) the Members.[23]

People who live and work inside the Beltway, such as politicos who run campaigns, think tanks, and advocacy groups in Washington, D.C., focus much of their attention on the differences between the candidates for the presidency (the *man* or woman). Given the outcome of the election, there has been a lot of talk about the ways Hillary Clinton was not a great candidate.[24] It is worth noting that plenty has also been written about how Donald Trump was a less than ideal candidate.[25] In *Activism, Inc.*, I discussed the dangers of relying on a charismatic candidate to win elections: "Only people with charisma can use it to their advantage, and it is unclear whether elected officials who win by means of charisma have strong political coattails."[26]

President Barack Obama, for example, was a charismatic leader with a strong message of change who mobilized a grassroots movement to secure his election in 2008, but his coattails proved to be quite short. During his eight years as president, the Democratic Party lost control of both houses of the U.S. Congress. This outcome is relatively common for sitting presidents, but the Democratic Party also lost control of statehouses around the country, which is much less common.[27] In March of 2017, Republicans controlled both chambers of the state legislature in thirty-two states, and Democrats controlled both chambers of the legislature in only fourteen states (three states split control and Nebraska is unicameral and nonpartisan).[28] In the words of Tim Dickinson in *Rolling Stone*, the eight years of the Obama presidency "papered over the fact that the party was being hollowed out from below. Over Obama's two terms, Democrats ceded 13 governorships to the GOP. . . . Across federal and state government, Democrats have lost close to 1,000 seats. There are only six states where Democrats control both the legislature and the governor's mansion."[29] Based on these trends through 2016, some critics pronounced the Democratic Party to be "in shambles in statehouses across the country."[30]

At the same time, the difference between the *messages* of the two candidates (and the implications of these differences) in the 2016 election was notable. Donald Trump's success involved a mix of factors; numerous accounts have discussed how the candidate succeeded, in part by promoting a message of status threat, which increased anxiety among high-status groups,[31] and by "mainstreaming resentment," which resonated with the white working class.[32] In contrast, the Clinton campaign was criticized for simplistic messaging focused on pointing out that a vote *for* candidate Clinton was a vote *against* Donald Trump.[33]

The message is important, and there were clear differences between candidates Trump and Clinton and their messages in 2016. But it is the *members* that matter; they are the voters—the political base of democracy in the United States. This aspect of politics is commonly referred to as the *grass roots*. This notion was borne of the idea that politics must be grounded in everyday citizens who are rooted in their localities. In contrast to the man or woman who runs for office and the message that his or her political campaign promotes, the members are not controllable by the campaign or the candidates. As much as political consultants focus on framing the message and capitalizing on an exceptionally charismatic candidate, it is still the opinions of the citizenry that decide elections.[34]

Barack Obama's 2008 campaign was renowned for its mobilization of grassroots supporters around the country. The campaign "trained some 3,000 full time organizers, most of them in their 20's; it organized thousands of local leadership teams . . . ; and it engaged some 1.5 million people in coordinated volunteer activity."[35] It employed an organizing strategy that cultivated the use of information communication technologies in innovative ways.[36] As Ari Melber put it, the Obama campaign was "the most wired supporter network in American history."[37] In fact, the 2008 campaign to elect Barack Obama president of the United States has been described by many as a *movement* and proof that the "bottom could prevail over the top."[38]

Even though many people, including me, interpreted the outcome of the 2008 election and the way the campaign connected with its members as a turning point for the Democratic Party,[39] no one predicted that the party would turn away from this model in future campaigns, relying on easier and less time-intensive options. In the introduction to their book on the Tea Party, in fact, Skocpol and Williamson discuss their attempt to compare the organization borne of the Obama Campaign—Organizing for America—to the Tea Party movement. After the 2008 election, "[Organizing for America] was essentially dormant at the grassroots, with phone banking and email alerts proceeding in ways typical of routine party politics."[40] Five years later, in the winter of 2017, Micah Sifry discussed how Obama's grassroots army was consolidated inside the Democratic Party. The implications of the decision to embed Organizing for America, which had access to the Obama campaign's 2.2 million members and 13 million email addresses, in the Democratic Party's infrastructure and entrust it to mainstream Democratic Party operatives were extensive. Sifry calls it the "seminal mistake" of the Obama presidency, "one that set the tone for the next eight years of dashed hopes, and helped pave the way for Donald Trump to harness the pent-up demand for change Obama had unleashed."[41]

The absorption of the Obama grassroots efforts into the Democratic Party also contributed directly to the clash between the Clinton and Sanders campaigns, which was one of the notable characteristics of the 2016 election. In the aftermath of the election, fissures within the party continued to be visible as the DNC struggled to name its new chair.[42] The distinction between the candidates for party chair were similar to the distinctions between candidates Sanders and Clinton. A main point of contention was how the party capitalized on the charisma of Barack Obama instead of working to engage members who had been empowered and engaged during the 2008 campaign. Party chair candidate Keith Ellison discussed the implications of the Democratic Party's (over)reliance on President Obama in January 2017 as a man and his message: "The tremendous popularity of Barack Obama, his amazing rhetorical skills, his just unparalleled ability to explain things and to inspire people really is the fuel that we lived on. Because of that, we lost a lot."[43]

Ellison's candidacy was supported by the more progressive leaders of the party, including Sanders, Elizabeth Warren, Chuck Schumer, and John Lewis. Nevertheless, he lost his bid to lead the Democratic Party to former secretary of Labor Tom Perez, whom some saw as representing the party establishment. Overall, the whole process was interpreted as a swipe at the more progressive side of the party.[44] The outcome of the race and the friction that has ensued provides clear evidence that the battle within the Democratic Party, which includes decisions about how to engage its members, is far from over.[45]

As the party continues to fight over its future, the Resistance has grown outside of it.[46] Although the Democratic Party tried to capitalize on the spirit and momentum of the Resistance to energize itself, it has been met with mixed reviews. In June 2017, Emily Cadei reported that "the DNC Wants to Join the Resistance. Will Activists Allow It?"[47] This *Newsweek* article summarized a number of efforts undertaken by the party to build on the momentum of the Resistance.

In the summer of 2017, a few weeks after MoveOn had introduced their "Resistance Summer" program, the Democratic Party launched its own campaign with the *same* name.[48] When I asked about what I thought was a collaboration with the Democratic Party, the organizing director at MoveOn set me straight: The DNC's program "was uncoordinated and not related to MoveOn . . . [it] represented the Democratic Party trying to keep pace with where the grassroots movement was and was going."[49] Given the Democratic Party's long-standing member problem, it makes sense that they would try to build on the Resistance's momentum. How this process played out in practice, however, was less positive. As Cadei concluded, "Party leaders may want to stick to the organizing nuts and bolts—and leave the splashy activism to Resistance groups."[50]

The Resistance began with one of the most common and visible social movement tactics—marching in the streets to protest—but it has employed a full range of tactics to target the Trump administration and its policies. This countermovement provides clear evidence of how social movements can blur the lines between issue-based activism and electoral work. In fact, the American Resistance provides extensive evidence that the distinction between "ballots and barricades" has blurred.[51] In *Deeply Divided*, Doug McAdam and Karina Kloos state that "the vast majority of social movements exert little or no effect on parties. In truth, most movements have no interest in engaging with parties or national politics more generally."[52] As I point out in detail, the American Resistance is not like most social movements. Since it began with the largest day of protest in U.S. history at the 2017 Women's March, the American Resistance has combined unconventional forms of contentious politics with more institutional forms of electoral politics to challenge the Trump administration and its policies.[53] Moreover, as I chronicle throughout the book, the American Resistance reverses the old wisdom about large demonstrations. Historically, demonstrations in Washington, D.C. were the final goal of local organizing, but today these large-scale demonstrations are part of the mobilization process rather than the conclusion of activism around specific issues.[54]

THE PROMISE OF DISTRIBUTED ORGANIZING

Beyond combining more confrontational tactics like protesting with institutional tactics like voting and lobbying, the Resistance is unique in the ways it employs distributed organizing to fill the gap left by a fragmented and ineffective Democratic

Party. As a 2016 Netroots Nation panel on the "mess and magic of distributed organizing" described it, *distributed organizing* involves "participatory campaigning" that is more bottom up and relies on technology to mobilize and connect people.[55] The heads of the distributed organizing team of the 2016 Bernie Sanders campaign described their experience this way: "The successful marriage of digital campaigning and volunteer field efforts in Bernie's distributed organizing combined aspects of old-school organizing practices with the social platforms that provide nearly constant mediation of the way people live and work in contemporary society."[56] This style of organizing is made possible by numerous digital tools that were developed, in part, by the Howard Dean and Barack Obama campaigns. To date, very little has been written about distributed organizing.[57]

In this book, I apply information gathered from conversations with individuals and groups working in multiple aspects of the Resistance to discuss three main characteristics of distributed organizing. First, membership is fluid and determined by interest, not action. Instead of requiring some sort of dues or service, members are defined as those who have shown interest by signing up through an event or on a list that is almost certainly digitally mediated.[58] As a result, people can be members of numerous groups simultaneously but may have a very limited connection to the group itself. David Karpf explained how membership has been subtly redefined as a "non-financial transaction." He observes that "MoveOn's 'members' often don't even know that they are members; they just know that they receive a lot of e-mails from the organization."[59] Based on my observations of groups participating in the Resistance, this claim is appropriate for most, if not all, of the groups engaging in distributed organizing today.

The second distinguishing characteristic of distributed organizing is that it no longer relies on the federated structure that had been the hallmark of American civil society organizations. In other words, most groups no longer derive strength and structure from connections among the federal, state, and local levels. This shift in the civic landscape did not begin with the Resistance. Harvard professor Theda Skocpol notes that America "originally became a nation of organizers and joiners of membership-based voluntary associations that operated in close symbiosis with representative government and democratic politics." However, civic groups no longer coalesce "into new (or renovated) omnibus federations able to link the grass roots to state, regional, and national leaderships, allowing longstanding American civic traditions to continue in new ways."[60]

Groups are embracing a distributed organizing model that does not even attempt to establish such a federated structure. Rather, civic groups are invested in actions at the local level that are loosely coordinated by national groups working as larger nodes in a relatively nonhierarchical network. Many of these locally embedded groups have no formal tax status or other administrative structures in place. The question that remains is this: Can a movement fueled by distributed organizing replace the federated structure that has eroded and left people bowling alone and campaigning without support in much of the country?[61]

Finally, this type of activism is no longer coordinated through brick-and-mortar offices with paid staff in communities. Even with a clear focus on social change at the local level, distributed organizing is geographically diffuse, and distributed activists are not necessarily situated where the work is being done. Few national Resistance groups reported having local offices. Rather, most coordination of local work is overseen by individuals who started informal groups in their localities or through field organizers working for national groups based outside the local area. Distributed organizing makes it possible for members to work through groups or alone—both are accepted and supported by national organizations.

Beyond being empowered to work individually, members are welcome to engage in their local communities or to participate from afar. My sister and I joined many other volunteers traveling to an adjacent swing district on the Last Weekend thanks to distributed organizing by numerous groups. Distributed organizing encourages members to channel their energies into other parts of the country if they are willing. It capitalizes on the energy of progressive Americans living in blue areas who are interested in doing more than just voting in their Democratic districts. The challenge of the geographic distances inherent to distributed organizing is how to connect geographically scattered activism with meaningful face-to-face connections among community members.

These three characteristics—fluid membership, loosely affiliated networks, and geographically diffuse organizing and activism—are made possible by the use of digital tools. Members and groups are connected through digital forms of communication, with the backbone being email lists, Slack channels, Facebook groups, and Twitter feeds that advertise events and, more often than not, ask for financial donations. Digital tools do more than just connect members and groups; they also facilitate all sorts of coordination.[62] Campaigns are curated by national groups that make "campaigns in a box" digitally available. These digital tools enable loosely connected groups to brand themselves and their work as part of an organization without much effort. Implementation of these campaigns and engagement with group members are determined by the loosely affiliated local networks of individuals and groups, not through national offices.

HOW AN UNYIELDING PRESIDENT TRUMP FANS THE FLAMES OF RESISTANCE

While the Resistance merges the momentum of some strong progressive social movements taking advantage of distributed organizing, it has also benefited from the moral outrage of Americans who were not previously politically engaged or connected. President Donald Trump and his way of communicating with the American public has motivated many to participate in democracy in America.[63] This shift in engagement is remarkable given the lull during the eight years of the Obama presidency, which asked very little of Left-leaning Americans beyond voting.[64] Since the 2016 election, however, progressives of all stripes have had much to yell about, and they have come out in droves: marching, chanting, and calling their elected officials regarding efforts made by the Trump administration around a range of progressive issues, including education, the environment, immigration, and health care. These high levels of civic engagement are in stark contrast to the disconnected base observed in the recent past.[65] It harkens back to the "good-ole-days" of the vibrant civic life of Americans.[66]

Among scholars of civic participation and social movements, there is a consensus that social networks—the connections to the people you know and organizations with whom you are affiliated—play an important role in mobilizing individuals to participate in all forms of civic activities, from voting to protesting to participating in organizations.[67] Social networks between friends and family play a huge role in mobilizing people to participate civically through social movements or political campaigns; social networks are the glue that connects many of us.[68] Although there is agreement that social ties provide much of the impetus to get us to participate, research has found that these social ties are weakening and that there is increasing social isolation in the United States.[69]

To understand the growth of the Resistance, it is important to look at the ways that disconnected individuals mobilize. In other words, what gets disconnected nonjoiners off their sofas and into the streets and town hall meetings? The answer is *moral shocks*: "when an event or situation raises such a sense of outrage in people that they become inclined toward political action, even in the absence of a network of contacts."[70] President Trump's utilization of the Congressional Review Act to undo the Obama legacy, his executive orders that include efforts to implement a travel ban, the exclusion of transgender people from serving in the U.S. military, and the U.S. withdrawal from the Paris Agreement on climate change, along with his vicious personal attacks via social media, have continually outraged a large proportion of the American public.[71] In many ways, the president's tactics build on what Jeffrey Berry and Sarah Sobieraj call the "Outrage Industry" of political media that involves "venom, vilification of opponents, and hyperbolic reinterpretations of current events."[72]

These moral shocks persisted throughout the Trump administration's first two years. Two weeks before the midterm elections in 2018, for example, the president tweeted: "Sadly, it looks like Mexico's Police and Military are unable to stop the Caravan heading to the Southern Border of the United States. Criminals and unknown Middle Easterners are mixed in. I have alerted Border Patrol and Military that this is a National Emergy (sic). Must change laws!"[73] Eleven days later, President Trump tweeted out a campaign ad that many called racist, employing what DNC chair Tom Perez described as "fear mongering" around the issue of immigration.[74] As a result of repeated moral shocks like these, the Resistance has expanded to include people already engaged in progressive politics as well as additional new blood that has been motivated to participate by outrage.

HOW DARK MONEY HAS LED TO
THE RESISTANCE

As the Democratic Party struggles and the president stokes outrage, the growing pull of dark money is changing U.S. politics. Thanks to the *Citizens United* decision in 2010, companies and individuals can advocate for or against candidates and issues through donations to tax-exempt social welfare groups and, in some cases, super PACs. Donations to these groups fall outside the spotlight of strict disclosure requirements regarding who gives candidates money and how they spend it, hence the name "dark money."[75] Although dark money donations span the political spectrum—including trade associations, social welfare groups, and unions—much of the focus is on funds from individual philanthropists and corporations supporting conservative causes and candidates. In fact, the *New York Times* editorial board made a direct connection between these funds and the Republican Party's success in the 2014 midterm elections with an op-ed titled "Dark Money Helped [the Republicans] Win the Senate."[76]

Since publication of *Dark Money* by Jane Mayer in January 2016, discussion has narrowed even further to focus on coordinated efforts led by the Koch brothers in specific federal, state, and local elections and campaigns.[77] One of the best known organizations to benefit from these funds is Americans for Prosperity, which has been credited with supporting winning conservative political candidates and blocking numerous progressive initiatives around health care, Medicaid, clean energy, and climate change.[78] One strategy this group employs is to support primary race opponents against incumbents who hold moderate positions on issues related to health care and the environment.[79] Mayer explains that dark money is "not just campaign money. It's a full-service operation."[80] Americans for Prosperity, along with a number of other groups actively connected to the Tea Party, benefited directly from resources made available through dark money. As Vanessa Williamson and colleagues note, dark money was "crucial to the funding of the Tea Party phenomenon at the national level."[81]

Although most of the critiques of dark money have been directed toward the political Right, dark money is increasingly common on the Left. One of the best known dark money contributors on the political Left is Tom Steyer, who spent millions through Next Generation during the 2016 election cycle.[82] In the summer before the 2016 election, this organization hired staffers from the Bernie Sanders presidential campaign to work on its 2016 efforts.[83] And Steyer is not alone. Many liberal donors, including George Soros and Michael Bloomberg, contributed dark money to super PACs and social welfare groups in attempts to sway the outcome of the 2016 election. In the fall of 2017, Steyer spent over $10 million to advertise a campaign to impeach President Trump.[84] These efforts on the political Right *and* Left give a small number of wealthy individuals even more power, consigning much of the power in our democracy to darkness and shadow.

LOOKING AT THE AMERICAN RESISTANCE

It is within this context—an out-of-touch Democratic Party; a president who is fanning the flames of racism, jingoism, and outrage; and the profound reach of wealthy donors' dark money—that the Resistance emerged. The Resistance has worked to keep *individuals*—many of whom are completely new to activism—engaged. To restate the well-known and potentially trite political adage: This movement is a marathon and not a sprint. For the Resistance to achieve its goals, individuals who have participated in protests in the streets must also participate in more sustained activism that employs a diversity of tactics. As we have learned from the civil rights movement, marching in the street on one Saturday (or even one Saturday a month) is not enough to create social change. The civil rights movement achieved its successes through sustained activism that included boycotts, freedom riders, and all sorts of nonviolent activism and protest.[85]

The first twenty-four months of the Trump administration saw extensive Resistance to the administration and its policies. In fact, so many acts of resistance occurred over this two-year period that they do not all fit on one figure. Figure 1.1 is a time line of the largest and what I consider to be the most politically salient protests since the inauguration of Donald Trump in January 2017. The figure clearly shows that protests continued

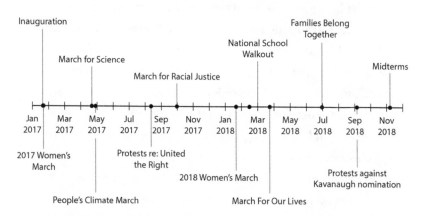

FIGURE 1.1 Resistance time line
Source: Author's own data.

to take place throughout the President's first two years in office. Given the frequency of protests, it is particularly important to diversify tactics to keep people engaged and involved. A long-term organizer who has planned large-scale protests in the United States since well before the 2016 election told me in fall 2017, "People are sick of marching on Washington."[86] Nevertheless, they persisted.

Protests and street demonstrations have been a well-known tactic of progressive political groups in the United States since at least the civil rights movement of the 1960s, but the organizations working to coordinate the efforts of individuals participating in the Resistance face numerous challenges. As can be seen from the cosponsors of the largest marches to date, these events were supported by coalitions of organizations that run the gamut in their levels of professionalization,[87] issue focus, and ideologies. The 2017 Women's March "partners," for example, included the Pussyhat Project, which shared knitting patterns for the infamous pink pussyhats; advocacy groups such as the National Organization for Women, the Sierra Club, and the National Bar Association; and unions, including the AFL-CIO and SEIU.[88] These groups include some unlikely bedfellows with long histories of competition,[89] but they will need to figure out ways to continue to work together for the Resistance to be successful and create long-term social change. In the chapters that follow, I document the Resistance, focusing on the individuals and the organizations that make up this unique movement.

It has been said that the Resistance began with the 2017 Women's March,[90] and chapter 2, "Resistance in the Streets," focuses on who is marching, what is motivating them to march, and what they are doing in addition to resisting in the streets. Research on social movements has looked at movement-to-movement transmission, but it has yet to explore the potentially overlapping motivations of participants who join social protests concentrated on one specific issue. In this chapter, I explore the overlapping motivations of the resistance in the streets, presenting evidence collected from the Resisters themselves.

Right after Donald Trump won the 2016 presidential election, two former congressional staffers got together to write a handbook to empower citizens in their communication with elected officials.[91] The *Indivisible Guide* was initially shared as a GoogleDoc via social media, and it outlined what its creators called a "Tea Party-Inspired Strategy" for targeting congresspeople in their districts. Since the handbook's release in December of 2016, Indivisible has grown rapidly, with many groups being formed on buses coming back from the 2017 Women's March.[92] As of November 2018, the Indivisible network included at least two groups in every congressional district in the United States.[93]

Chapter 3, "Organizing the Resistance in the Districts," documents how political groups including Indivisible worked to shift the resistance in the streets into resistance in the districts. Since the inauguration, town hall meetings with elected officials throughout the United States have been flooded by constituents turning out *en masse* to discuss immigration policy and health care reform, among many other issues. These meetings have sometimes overflowed onto the streets, and some elected officials have even refused to attend them. In this chapter, interview data collected from the leaders of Resistance groups illustrate how these groups are employing distributed organizing to get the job done. It highlights the strength of this unlikely coalition of partners and the challenges they face.

Chapter 4, "Resistance in the Districts," traces the efforts of participants in the resistance in the streets into their work as part of the resistance in the districts. In this chapter, I focus on how participants in the resistance in the streets channeled their outrage into specific efforts at the local and congressional district level. Using data collected through follow-up surveys with Resisters, I assess how these individuals worked with organizations to affect social change, which groups they worked with, and what they did. I look specifically at the degree to which resistance in the districts was facilitated by the work of Resistance groups and the Democratic Party. I also describe the top issues Resisters believe we are facing today, what they think are the best solutions to these problems, and discuss how those opinions changed during the period of my study.

Chapter 5, "Looking Back While Marching Forward," summarizes what the Resistance looks like two years later. I synthesize the findings from other chapters and explore what we can expect from the Resistance going forward. I begin in the streets, describing the third Women's March in January 2019, and look at how the American Resistance is likely to carry on following the midterm elections. I conclude with a discussion of what we can expect from the Resistance as the 2020 election cycle gets under way, and what the potential outcomes of that election will mean for the Resistance and for the resurgence of democratic participation in America.

Chapter Two

RESISTANCE IN THE STREETS

A SINGLE piano began to play as singer Andra Day walked across the stage in front of the Cardinal Shehan Children's Choir from Baltimore. The kids were wearing school uniforms with red sweaters, but the singer was dressed in black with a fur coat draped off one of her shoulders. Her voice flowed out over the hundreds of thousands of people standing on Pennsylvania Avenue on this overcast spring day:

> I'll rise up, I'll rise unafraid
> I'll rise up, And I'll do it a thousand times again.

As the chorus rang out and Day's voice pierced the din of the crowd, eight hundred thousand people quieted and swayed along with the woman who had been tasked with beginning the March For Our Lives. The two people taking my survey froze and stared with their mouths open as her voice swelled and the children sang along. Even my eleven-year-old daughter, who had pleaded to help me survey the crowd in her new pink pussyhat but had started begging me to buy her food within the first hour, stopped and stared. In eighteen years of surveying protesters in large crowds, I had never seen anything like it.

I've been studying activism by surveying protesters in the streets at demonstrations since 2000. I have surveyed thousands of participants at protest events around North America and Europe. Protesters corrected my pronunciation in Paris at the Youth Labor Law (CPE) protests in 2006; I avoided tear gas during the Another World Is Possible March at the 2002 World Economic Forum in New York City; and it took a week to get feeling back in my toes after I surveyed protesters at the Copenhagen Climate March in December of 2009.

For me, it all started in the Hague at the Human Dike protest during the 2000 climate negotiations. I was in the Netherlands collecting some final data for my dissertation comparing national responses to the climate regime.[1] Having worked for NGOs that focused on citizen responses to environmental policies previously, I was fascinated by the large-scale protest event called for the weekend during the negotiations. Much of the research on activism around international events had overlooked the individuals who participate in these protests. To understand who came out and why they were participating, I put together a short survey. With the help of a friend who was also a graduate student, we administered the survey to 204 participants randomly selected throughout the crowd as they filled sandbags and built a dike around the conference center where the negotiations were taking place.

At the end of the event, the environment minister from the Netherlands joined the crowd and placed the last sandbag on top of the "Human Dike" that had been formed. As journalists' cameras clicked all around him, I realized that contemporary protest was very different from what I had learned about social movements in graduate school. Large-scale mobilizations like the Human Dike are used by political actors working both outside *and* inside institutional politics to express the will of the people.[2] The goal of events like this one is to mobilize participants in a way that is both visibly compelling and instills a sense of collective identity.[3] When a demonstration mobilizes a large crowd and is picked up by the media, images of the event provide media consumers (otherwise known as "the public") with an indication either that a critical mass supports the goals of the organizers, in the best cases, or that the people protesting are just a bunch of hooligans who want to destroy property, in the worst cases. People may be demonstrating against specific policies—such as the war in Iraq or the USA Patriot Act— or may be marching to encourage a policy—such as a stronger international agreement to regulate greenhouse gas emissions. Some demonstrations support government actions, and others are meant to oppose them.[4]

When the first Women's March was called after the 2016 election, I knew I had to get back into the streets to observe the event and collect data from the participants. The call to march on the day after the inauguration sparked a lot of interest, and information about it was spreading like wildfire over social media.[5] I joined forces with two of my colleagues whose research focuses on race in America, and we worked together to update my survey based on what we expected to see on the day after the inauguration.[6] Given the recent success of events coordinated by Occupy Wall Street, Black Lives Matter, and the climate movement, the march had the potential to mobilize participants with varying concerns across the progressive spectrum.[7] We believed that the march might turn out a crowd motivated by issues that spanned race, class, gender, and sexual orientation. To answer these questions, our survey was designed to collect data about the diversity of the crowd and the diversity of the motivations that drew people to join the first Women's March.

The enthusiasm on social media translated into real world fervor, and the 2017 Women's March mobilized approximately four million people around the country, becoming the largest protest in U.S. history.[8] As I surveyed participants in front of the Hirshhorn Museum, I bumped into many people from various stages of my own life: a woman I hadn't seen since high school graduation, my ex-boyfriend from college marching with his wife, a guy from my PhD program in Wisconsin, and many people from my life as a professor in the Washington, D.C. area.

Although protests against Donald Trump had been relatively common during his campaign for president, the Resistance as a movement did not really start until his presidency formally began. In fact, the Women's March has been called the "trigger" of the Resistance.[9] Since then, protest events have taken place around the United States focusing on a variety of issues, including racial justice, climate change, immigration, and the Trump administration's perceived stance on science. In most cases, the main location for these marches has been Washington, D.C.

where people can march by the White House (or encircle it as they did at the People's Climate March in April 2017).

Much speculation has revolved around who attended the Women's March and subsequent demonstrations in the Resistance, as well as what issues motivated these individuals to raise their voices in protest. In this chapter, I analyze a unique data set collected from a random sample of participants from the largest protests since Trump's inauguration to understand who participated in the resistance in the streets and why these individuals chose to protest President Trump and his policies. I begin with an overview of the resistance in the streets, then briefly describe the events included in my analysis. Finally, I discuss my findings from surveying participants at these events to further our understanding of who has participated in the resistance in the streets and where the movement is headed.

STUDYING THE RESISTANCE IN THE STREETS

My goal was to study all the "big" protests of the Resistance. To achieve that goal, I needed to determine what, exactly, constituted a large protest. I decided only to study events for which at least twenty-five thousand people turned out to stand, yell, and (maybe) march in Washington, D.C. Although this size criterion is an arbitrary number, given the frequency of protests during this period, a threshold for inclusion was needed to make the project possible. Despite the high number of protest events since Trump took office, only a few demonstrations have included at least twenty-five thousand people in Washington,

D.C.: the Women's Marches in 2017 and 2018, the March for Science, the People's Climate March, the March For Our Lives, and the Families Belong Together event. In addition to these six events, I present data collected from the March for Racial Justice, which took place in September 2017.

To understand the makeup of these crowds, it is necessary to collect a defensible sample of participants—that is, a random sample from throughout the staging area—so the findings can be interpreted as representative of the population of the protest more generally.[10] All of the data presented in this chapter were collected by surveying protesters in a manner consistent with my previous research on protest events going back to the Human Dike in the Netherlands in 2000.[11] Over the years, I have worked with research teams, many of whom were undergraduate and graduate students, to walk through demonstrations at regular increments, administering surveys as we snake through the frequently crowded staging areas where people wait to hear speeches and line up to march. We attempt to sample every fifth person. We ask them to participate, and if they agree, we survey them (see appendix for survey details). Everyone collects about the same number of surveys from his or her section of the crowd; and when combined, this sample provides a reasonable snapshot of who was in the streets on a given day. Although the protesting populations at each event are unique in some ways, a consistent pattern across participants emerges. In other words, these data tell us a lot about who is participating in the Resistance.

In this chapter, I present data collected from participants at all seven of these events, whom I call *Resisters*. Taken together, the responses to my surveys include data from 1,929 participants at the largest protest events to take place in Washington, D.C. since the inauguration of Donald Trump. I focus on who has been marching in the streets, what mobilized them, and what else they are doing in addition to participating in demonstrations.

GATHERING DATA ON THE RESISTANCE IN THE STREETS

I surveyed events in Washington, D.C., but each of these events included sibling marches in other U.S. cities (and in some cases around the world).[12] Simultaneous activism in multiple locations has been a component of protests at least since 1999 when the antiglobalization movement began coordinating events internationally.[13] However, the structure of current protest events is a hallmark of activism in an age of distributed organizing, which capitalizes on coordination using digital tools. It is now possible to organize central events as well as to provide online toolkits so activists can create events anywhere. Many of these events were coordinated through conference calls and huddles.[14] Table 2.1 presents an overview of the turnout of each march, as well as the data collected from participants and the refusal rate at each event.

THE WOMEN'S MARCH 2017

The Women's March was formed in response to a series of individual calls to action on Facebook. A group of women who had never met (including a white grandmother in Hawaii who

TABLE 2.1 Overview of survey data from each march

	Women's March 2017	March for Science	People's Climate March	March for Racial Justice	Women's March 2018	March For Our Lives	Families Belong Together
Estimated attendance	750,000	100,000	200,000	10,000	75,000	800,000	35,000
Total completed surveys	530	201	351	185	205	256	201
Response rate	92%	94%	89%	83%	92%	93%	91%

Source: Author's own data.

got a lot of press) worked together to become a broad, intersectional coalition of seasoned activists that mobilized what has been called "the largest single-day demonstration in recorded U.S. history." The march in Washington, D.C. was part of a day of action that took place in 653 places around the United States, with 261 other events taking place around the globe. Chenoweth and Pressman report that about four million people turned out to events in the United States.[15]

As participants flooded the same streets that had hosted the inaugural parade only twenty-four hours earlier, chants opposing the new administration reverberated through the air. An estimated 750,000 people descended on Washington, D.C. to participate in the Women's March. Thanks to efforts by the Pussyhat Project, many in the crowd had a uniform look as a sea of pink hats flooded the streets.[16] Organizers of the march had secured a list of high-profile speakers, including Gloria Steinem and Madonna. Given the size of the crowd and technical difficulties with the jumbotrons positioned along the mall, the majority of us in the crowd could neither see nor hear the speakers during the event. In fact, only one of the eight members of my research team (who was collecting data at the front of the crowd) was able to see the stage and hear any of the speeches and performers.

As I walked through the crowd with a set of clipboards, I was constantly asked where the toilets were and when and where we were going to march. When I explained that I was there to survey the crowd and had no connection to the organizers or the plans for the day, many people volunteered to take the survey. I explained that they hadn't been randomly sampled and, thus, could not participate. I also pointed out that the march was planned without a staging area, so the 750,000-person crowd would have had to march through itself to move. Organizers could have tried to get the massive crowd to part, but not without risking "crowd crush" (or what everyday people might refer to as a stampede). Getting the Women's March to march could have risked the safety of its participants, so in the end the Women's March didn't march anywhere. It just stood still, and the organizers explained that the Women's March didn't march because they were "too big to march."

THE MARCH FOR SCIENCE

In contrast to the Women's March, which was started on Facebook, the March for Science began with a "throwaway line on Reddit." Its aim was "to defend the role of science in policy and society."[17] Although it was originally proposed on social media, the march took on a number of professional scientific associations as its partners, including the American Association for the Advancement of Science and a number of social scientific professional groups including the American Sociological Association.[18] Numerous claims proclaimed that the march mobilized a new group of scientist-activists who have the potential to be channeled into innovative forms of political action.[19] However, analysis of the data collected at the march shows that there were few differences between the makeup of this march and other marches in the Resistance.[20]

Like the Women's March, satellite marches were reported with more than six hundred events around the United States and throughout the world. In total, more than a million people turned out, and the flagship March for Science in Washington, D.C., which was held on Earth Day, April 22, 2017, included one hundred thousand people marching in the rain. Similar to the Women's March, the event involved a rally with speeches. In this case, the speakers included notable scientists. Even though it was pouring rain by the time headliner Bill Nye "the science guy" took the stage, he was welcomed like a rock star with cheers erupting throughout the soggy crowd.[21]

PEOPLE'S CLIMATE MARCH 2017

The People's Climate March was held in Washington, D.C. on April 29, 2017, exactly one week after the March for Science and on President Trump's one hundredth day in office. This event was a follow-up to the first People's Climate March, which took place in New York City three years earlier on the Sunday before the United Nations held talks on the issue of climate change. This march was connected to a broader effort to draw attention to the issue of climate change in the United States, and it was unique in not being a direct response to the Trump administration and its policies. Participants had plenty to protest by late April 2017, however, and people turned out to express their concerns about the environmental agenda of the Trump administration.[22] President Trump had signed an executive order in March rescinding the Clean Power Plan and was threatening to pull out of the Paris Agreement on climate change (which he did formally in June 2017). Like the Women's March and the March for Science, and the 2014 People's Climate March, this event coincided with more than 370 coordinated protests around the United States.[23]

Even though more than one hundred thousand people had turned out for the soggy March for Science the previous weekend, an estimated two hundred thousand people participated in the climate-focused event in Washington, D.C. on an unseasonably hot and sunny April day, with temperatures over 90 degrees matching the heat record. Many famous people were rumored to be in the crowd. In fact, one member of the research team surveyed in the area where Virgin Atlantic CEO Richard Branson was holding court. Sadly, he was not randomly selected to be a part of the sample. Although photos also placed Leonardo DiCaprio at the front of the crowd, no one from the research team ever caught a glimpse of him in the staging area. Protesters in Washington, D.C. marched to the White House, and in a stunning display of collective action, the crowd circled the White House at the end of the march to show that the world was watching.[24]

MARCH FOR RACIAL JUSTICE

Like the Women's March and the March for Science, the March for Racial Justice was also initiated by a less institutionalized actor. In contrast to these other marches, however, the March for Racial Justice was not coordinated by a diverse national committee of seasoned activists, nor did it connect with a broad coalition of national groups as organizational partners. On September 30, 2017, the March for Racial Justice was held in Lincoln Park near Capitol Hill. The protest was planned in

June after a police officer was acquitted in the death of Philando Castile in Minnesota. After the president's response to the killing of a peaceful protester by a white supremacist in Charlottesville, Virginia, in August and his September critiques of NFL athletes who had taken a knee during the national anthem to express their concern about police brutality and their desire for racial justice in America, many expected the march to gain additional support.[25] The march was scheduled to take place on the same day as the March for Black Women, which was held a few blocks from the staging area of the March for Racial Justice. After separate rallies took place, the two groups converged and marched together toward the Capitol and the Department of Justice, ending at the National Mall. A number of concurrent events took place around the country.[26]

Due in part to its lack of institutional support, turnout was much lower than that for the other marches in Washington, D.C. An estimated ten thousand people participated in the march, which included people from both rallies.

THE WOMEN'S MARCH 2018

The national Women's March group decided to celebrate the one-year anniversary of the march with a rally in Las Vegas, Nevada, in January 2018, However, many of the organizers of the sister marches that had taken place around the country in 2017, as well as a newer group called March On and local nodes of Indivisible, chose to commemorate the anniversary with another march.[27] After some tense interactions among groups involved in the 2017 Women's March, the 2018 Women's March was held on the weekend of the anniversary (January 20–21, 2018) in 407 locations, and an estimated two million people turned out around the United States.[28]

The march in Washington, D.C. in 2018 was organized by March Forward Virginia, "the [Virginia] state-level organizers for the 2017 Women's March." The event was originally arranged to showcase the numerous women's successes that had taken place in 2017 in Virginia. However, because Congress failed to come to a budget agreement, the federal government had just shut down the night before the march took place. As a result, many democratic leaders stayed in Washington that weekend, attending the march and speaking at the rally.[29] An estimated seventy-five thousand people participated in the second Women's March in Washington, D.C.

MARCH FOR OUR LIVES

In contrast to the other demonstrations, which had been organized by adults, but it was the high school students who had survived the school shooting in Parkland, Florida—who organized the March For Our Lives. With the help of some well-resourced benefactors, including Oprah Winfrey and George Clooney, the March For Our Lives rally was held in Washington, D.C. on March 24, a mere six weeks after the school shooting February 14. The event included speeches by survivors of gun violence and performances by musicians, including pop stars Demi Lovato, Ariana Grande, Andra Day, and *Hamilton* creator Lin-Manuel Miranda. The march in Washington, D.C. was supported by 763 sibling marches around the country. Organizers estimate that eight hundred thousand people attended the event in Washington, D.C., and the day of action turned out an estimated 1.5 million people around the United States.[30]

For the first time, my eleven-year-old daughter joined me at the march as an observer. There's no doubt that the students' call to action, coupled with the impressive lineup of performers, got her excited about attending the march. In contrast to the 2017 Women's March, where we couldn't hear anything happening on the main stage, the March For Our Lives placed jumbotrons all along Pennsylvania Avenue, and anyone near the wide street could see the concert and hear it. The size of the crowd was intimidating; trying to cross Pennsylvania Avenue with my daughter to meet the research team was the first time in eighteen years that I ever felt panicky in a crowd I was studying. As we tried to cross the street without being separated, Ariana Grande was projected on the jumbotrons along the broad street, and people continued to pour out of the metro and push their way down to Pennsylvania Avenue to see the concert. It took us more than twenty minutes to cross the street and get out of the crush.

FAMILIES BELONG TOGETHER

The other events had been organized months (or weeks in the case of the March For Our Lives) ahead of time, but the Families Belong Together event was organized in just twelve days to protest the Trump administration's family separation policy that led to migrant children being separated from their parents and held for prosecution. The event was led by a diverse coalition of more than one hundred organizations, including MoveOn, the American Civil Liberties Union, the National Domestic Workers Alliance, and the Leadership Conference on Civil and Human Rights.[31] In total, about 450,000 people turned out around the United States to protest the Trump administration's separation of migrant children from their parents. The flagship event was in Washington, D.C., and there were 738 sibling marches.[32]

An estimated thirty-five thousand people turned out in the sweltering summer heat in Washington, D.C. to listen to speeches and march.[33] Once again, Lin-Manuel Miranda performed. As I surveyed the crowd on Lafayette Square right next to the White House, he sang the song "Dear Theodosia" from *Hamilton* a cappella. During the chorus, the crowd joined in singing the song with Miranda as a duet: "I'll do whatever it takes; I'll make the world safe and sound for you." As I waited for people to complete their surveys, the song rang out all around me. I joined the thousands of voices singing along; everyone knew every word.

WHO IS PARTICIPATING IN RESISTANCE IN THE STREETS?

The demographics of participants in these seven marches is remarkably similar and was dominated by highly educated women who are about forty years old. At every event, more women turned out than men, which is consistent with other studies of participation in the Resistance.[34] This finding stands in sharp contrast to earlier research that found men were more likely to participate in protests in the civil rights movement, and more recent work that found no significant differences in protest participation by gender.[35]

The resistance in the streets is mobilizing highly educated crowds: one-third of the U.S. population has a bachelor's degree,[36] but more than two-thirds of the participants at each event held a bachelor's degree or higher. Among the large-scale protests in Washington, D.C. since the Resistance began, my research found that the March for Science mobilized the highest percentage of doctors, lawyers, and scientists (21 percent),[37] the Families Belong Together march in June 2018 had the highest percentage of participants who had completed a master's degree (56 percent), and the 2017 Women's March had the highest percentage of participants with a bachelor's degree or higher (87 percent).

In contrast to those who claim that millennials are the "foot soldiers of the Resistance,"[38] the resistance in the street at these seven events was not a particularly young crowd. The average age of participants ranged from thirty-eight at the March for Racial Justice to forty-nine at the March For Our Lives.[39] In her analysis of generational spillover in the Resistance, Whittier analyzed the data we collected at the 2017 Women's March. She noted that attendees were relatively evenly divided across generations, underscoring that millennials were not disproportionately engaged.[40]

The most significant demographic differences across the protest events can be seen in the racial and ethnic makeup of each event. Although all events turned out predominantly white crowds, the racial/ethnic distribution of those who identified as nonwhites varied by protest event (see table 2.2). The lowest participation of nonwhites was at the March for Science, which focused specifically on science-related issues: 80 percent of the participants were white, only 1 percent were black, and 10 percent identified as multiracial. The highest percentage of black participation (18 percent) was at the March for Racial Justice, with 7 percent identifying as multiracial. The highest percentage of Latinx participation (9 percent) was at the Families Belong Together event, with 8 percent identifying as multiracial. These findings are not particularly surprising because events explicitly focused on identity-based issues, such as racial justice or immigration rights, are expected to mobilize the people most likely to experience these issues. Overall, the percentage of white participants was relatively stable and similar to the national averages for college-educated Americans.[41]

THE POLITICS OF THE RESISTANCE IN THE STREETS

As expected, the resistance in the streets is overwhelmingly progressive in its political orientation (see table 2.3). The majority of participants at every event identified as Left-leaning, with the average response at every march placing participants somewhere between Left and slightly Left-leaning.[42] The March For Our Lives had a somewhat higher proportion of self-identified moderates than the other marches.[43] In addition, most Resisters

TABLE 2.2 Demographics of the Resistance in the streets (in percent)

	Women's March 2017	March for Science	People's Climate March	March for Racial Justice	Women's March 2018	March For Our Lives	Families Belong Together
Gender							
Female	85	54	57	66	78	70	71
Male	14	42	41	32	17	29	27
Other	1	4	2	2	2	2	2
Educational attainment							
Bachelor's degree	34	35	35	30	36	36	28
Graduate degree	53	47	42	40	38	36	56
Total bachelor's degree or higher	87	82	77	70	75	72	84
Race/ethnicity							
White	77	80	77	62	77	78	70
Latinx	4	4	6	7	3	5	9
Black	7	1	3	18	9	8	7
Asian	4	5	6	6	7	3	5
Multiracial/other	8	10	6	7	5	6	8

Source: Author's own data.

TABLE 2.3 Politics of the Resistance in the streets (in percent)

	Women's March 2017	March for Science	People's Climate March	March for Racial Justice	Women's March 2018	March For Our Lives	Families Belong Together
Political ideology/voting							
Left	92	83	86	87	85	79	87
Moderate, middle of the road	6	10	7	7	11	16	8
Right	1	5	2	4	4	3	3
Voted for Hillary Clinton	90	84	82	79	85	89	89
Protest experience							
First-timers	33	30	24	18	16	27	9
Attended Women's March 2017	*	46	70	76	79	78	75
Attended March for Science	*	*	34	34	41	28	31
Attended People's Climate March	*	*	*	25	26	19	22
Attended March for Racial Justice	*	*	*	*	17	8	21
Attended Women's March 2018					*	51	51
Attended March For Our Lives						*	56

Source: Author's own data.

*Data were collected at the time of the survey.

reported having voted for Hillary Clinton for president in 2016 (ranging from a low of 79 percent of participants at the March for Racial Justice to a high of 90 percent of participants at the 2017 Women's March).

Although the resistance in the streets was overwhelmingly women who were Clinton supporters, many participants reported being completely new to the experience of protesting. Thirty-three percent of all participants at the 2017 Women's March and 30 percent of participants at the March for Science reported never having participated in a protest. This percentage is particularly notable because it is higher than the percentage of novices at demonstrations from other recent studies.[44] In general, fewer new protesters are joining the Resistance at each event.[45]

The diminishing number of new protest participants at each event must be understood within the context of the broader resistance in the streets (what some scholars refer to as a "cycle of contention"[46]), which involves a sustained response to the Trump administration and its policies. To that end, the percentage of repeat Resisters who have participated in the events that make up the resistance in the streets has been very high at every event. In fact, three-quarters of all participants at the March for Racial Justice, the 2018 Women's March, the March For Our Lives, and the Families Belong Together event also reported attending the 2017 Women's March.[47] The high level of repeat protesting, or what some scholars refer to as differential participation or persistence, is particularly remarkable because these people are participating in events that focus on very different issues within a single two-year period.[48] There is no reason to expect people who marched for women's rights to turn out to march for science, for the climate, or for gun control. Nevertheless, they are; those who have joined the Resistance are turning out to march again and again.

WHAT IS MOTIVATING THE RESISTANCE IN THE STREETS

Why are people participating in such a range of protest events? To understand what motivated participants to join these events, my colleagues and I did something relatively novel—we asked them. Although including this question may seem obvious, only limited research has looked at the potentially overlapping motivations among protest participants.[49] If you come out for a Women's March, most studies of protest tend to assume that you were motivated to attend by having an interest in women's issues, or you're a general joiner looking for something to do on a Saturday.[50] To test this assumption, we asked everyone we surveyed to answer this question: "What issues motivated you to participate today?"[51]

By directly asking Resisters what motivated them to join, we were also able to look at the degree to which they were motivated by intersectional interests—identity-based interests that have been found to cross race, class, gender, sexual orientation, legal status, and other categories of identity.[52] Some scholars have suggested that these intersections divide people into silos characterized by distinct and competing interests that prevent the kind of coalition building necessary for strong social movement organizing.[53] But intersectional interests can be used to build coalitions within and across social movements.[54] As a result, this strategy increases the number and diversity of activists, promoting coalitions rather than divisions.[55]

At the 2017 Women's March, respondents listed an average of 2.8 reasons they were motivated to march, and their responses ran the gamut. Some participants focused specifically on their individual identity/identities. For example, one respondent wrote: "(1) my parents are immigrants, (2) I'm Mexican-American, (3) I'm a woman, (4) my boyfriend is Muslim, (5) I feel personally attacked by Trump's presidency and his Twitter." Others were more focused on politics: "Trump's beliefs and behaviors, equal pay, single payer, control of the Supreme Court, women's rights." In some instances, participants' political motivations included expressions that reflected their outrage: "The defunding of planned parenthood as well as women's rights being shitted on by an orange man."

The responses from all 530 surveyed participants were coded into fourteen categories: women's rights; reproductive rights; environment; lesbian, gay, bisexual, transgender, and queer (LGBTQ) issues; racial justice; police brutality; immigration; religion; social welfare; labor; peace; equality; politics/voting; and President Trump. Participants at every event following the 2017 Women's March were asked the same question, but instead of writing in their answers, respondents checked off which of the fourteen categories that had emerged at the Women's March motivated them (for more details, see appendix). Respondents who responded to this "check-off" option provided more answers overall, but the average number of motivations varied by event: 5 motivations per participant at the March for Science, 5.5 at the People's Climate March, 6.3 at the March for Racial Justice, 9.5 at the 2018 Women's March, 4.5 at the March For Our Lives, and 6.4 at the Families Belong Together event. Even with these differences, it is clear that multiple issues drove individuals to participate in each march.[56]

Table 2.4 presents the motivations of participants at all of the marches. As expected, the named focus of each event received the highest responses: women's rights was the most common motivation for participants at the Women's March (61 percent in 2017 and 92 percent in 2018); the environment was the most common motivation for participants at the March for Science (93 percent) and the People's Climate March (97 percent); racial justice was the most common motivation at the March for Racial Justice (89 percent); social welfare (which includes gun control) was the most common motivation at the March For Our Lives (57 percent); and immigration was the most common motivation for participants at the Families Belong Together event (96 percent). Participants also reported being motivated by other reasons that spanned the progressive spectrum. For example, participants in the Women's March also reported being motivated by the environment (36 percent), racial justice (35 percent), LGBTQ issues (35 percent), and reproductive rights (33 percent).

Perhaps due to the actions of President Trump and his administration, secondary motivations at events that took place after the 2017 Women's March went up overall.[57] More than 40 percent of participants at the March for Science reported being motivated by women's rights (40 percent), equality (45 percent),

TABLE 2.4 Motivations of participants across the Resistance in the streets (in percent)

Motivation of participants	Women's March 2017	March for Science	People's Climate March	March for Racial Justice	Women's March 2018	March For Our Lives	Families Belong Together
Environment	36	93	97	22	67	20	22
Equality	25	45	47	75	89	30	65
Immigration	22	29	34	58	78	19	96
LGBTQ	35	22	28	41	67	19	29
Labor	12	19	25	20	46	8	23
Peace	20	35	43	42	66	54	51
Police brutality/Black Lives Matter	18	22	29	80	59	36	34
Politics/voting	16	44	39	37	73	48	48
Racial justice	35	26	36	89	76	31	65
Religion	9	13	17	13	25	9	14
Reproductive rights	33	32	28	24	73	15	28
Social welfare (includes guns and health care)	23	35	37	39	63	57	44
President Trump	29	53	56	44	72	49	58
Women's rights	61	40	40	48	92	33	47

Source: Author's own data.

politics/voting (44 percent), and President Trump (53 percent). At the People's Climate March the following weekend, 56 percent of the crowd reported being motivated by President Trump, 47 percent were motivated by issues related to equality, 43 percent reported being motivated by peace, and 40 percent reported being motivated by women's rights. Participants at the March for Racial Justice, in contrast, were very motivated by identity-based issues. At least 80 percent of participants reported being motivated by police brutality and 75 percent by equality, and 58 percent also reported being motivated by immigration. At the 2018 Women's March, which took place during the first day of a government shutdown, every motivation was high. The only motivations that received *less than* 50 percent were labor (46 percent) and religion (25 percent). At the March For Our Lives two months later, the crowd expressed very different motivations.[58] Many new people participated who were not motivated by the topic of the march; 54 percent reported being motivated by peace, 49 percent by President Trump, and 48 percent by politics/voting. Motivations were even higher at the Families Belong Together event in the summer of 2018,[59] with 65 percent of participants motivated by racial justice and equality, and 58 percent motivated by President Trump. These results clearly show that participants in the resistance in the streets are not aligning exclusively with one specific issue; rather, they are motivated by many intersecting and overlapping issues.

Along with colleagues, I have looked at intersectionality in the Resistance by specifically analyzing the overlapping motivations of protest participants. We found that "individuals' motivations to participate [in the Women's March] represented an intersectional set of issues" showing explicitly "how coalitions of issues emerge."[60] More recently, we compared the overlapping motivations across participants who turned out at all of the events in 2017—from the 2017 Women's March through the March for Racial Justice—and looked at the degree to which consistent patterns of motivations appeared at each protest event. We found that "although many participants held intersectional motivations across race, gender, class, and sexuality, the patterns of these overlapping motivations are not particularly durable; they are different among participants at every march."[61] These results provide clear evidence that the motivations that mobilize individuals to participate in the resistance in the streets change over time and from one event to another. The Trump administration has been administering moral shocks to progressive Americans on a regular basis through executive orders; proposed policies on immigration, health care, the environment, and racial justice; and many other issues, along with personal attacks via social media.[62] In this climate, it is not surprising that motivations among Resisters have shifted quickly.

RESISTING OFF THE STREETS

As a countermovement, the Resistance is expected to continue to evolve as the targets shift in response to actions by the Trump administration. These ups and downs in the resistance in the streets are consistent with previous social movements that employed a suite of tactics to respond to oppression.[63] In his well-known work on the civil rights movement, Aldon Morris provides clear evidence of how the varied organizational forces contributed to the tactics and timing of the struggle to end segregation.[64] Similarly, as I discuss in more detail in chapter 3, the organizations that are helping to coordinate the Resistance are combining the tactic of marching in the streets with other tactics that they believe are most appropriate. To repeat the response given to me by a long-time organizer who has worked on mass mobilizations (including the 2017 Women's March) when I asked him in fall 2017 if turnout in marches would continue to be high, he said: "People are sick of marching on Washington."[65] Nevertheless, they have continued to turn out again and again.[66]

Many of the people we surveyed in the streets were already civically engaged. Overall, even though there are some differences among the participants in the resistance in the streets, the levels of civic engagement among march participants were relatively stable across fourteen measures of engagement. Participation was quite high regarding two actions that have been encouraged by many groups working to channel the Resistance into the communities where activists live and work (see table 2.5). More than half of the Resisters at all of the events reported contacting an elected official in the past year, ranging from 58 percent at the 2017 Women's March to 72 percent at the Families Belong Together event in July 2018. Participation in town hall meetings was also high; more than 40 percent of participants at all of the events reported attending a town hall meeting in the past year. In fact, the percentage reporting attending a town hall meeting went up at each event in 2017, suggesting that people who were participating in the resistance

TABLE 2.5 Civic engagement beyond Resistance in the streets (in percent)

In the past year, have you . . .	Women's March 2017	March for Science	People's Climate March	March for Racial Justice	Women's March 2018	March For Our Lives	Families Belong Together
Contacted elected official	58	63	70	65	61	61	72
Attended town hall meeting	42	43	48	52	41	41	51
Contacted the media to express a view	21	15	30	27	20	17	21
Participated in direct action	23	31	41	41	28	22	41
Worn a safety pin for social justice	31	25	21	33	37	27	30

Source: Author's own data.

in the streets were increasingly taking their Resistance into their congressional districts as well. In 2018, the numbers fluctuated as many members of Congress decided not to hold town hall meetings.[67]

In an analysis to understand who is turning out again and again, the variables that explain persistence in the Resistance are surprising.[68] In particular, having contacted an elected official in the past year is a significant predictor of persistence in this movement. This finding is in contrast to the variables that explained longer-term protest experience prior to the Resistance. It provides additional evidence that people who are turning out to protest the Trump administration and its policies are not just engaging in confrontational tactics; they are also participating in institutional politics in their congressional districts.

The issue of reproductive rights has also motivated people to turn out again and again. This finding replicates what other studies of protests in the Resistance have found: Women and women's issues have been a major focus of the current cycle of contention since the 2017 Women's March.[69] This finding also provides more evidence that the Women's March and the issues it focused on was the spark that ignited the Resistance.[70] Politics/voting was negatively associated with persistence. Some people came out to participate in demonstrations because they were motivated by their concerns about the political system in the United States—such as gerrymandering or voter suppression—but they were less likely to come out again and again.

SUMMARY

I have presented an analysis of the participants in the resistance in the streets in this chapter. Resisters are highly educated, predominantly female, and mostly white. They are Left-leaning and civically engaged. Many have participated in this form of Resistance again and again. Resisters are motivated by a range of progressive issues, and they have taken to the streets to express their opinions and to show their strength. In chapter 3, I look at the groups that are working with resisters as they take on activities in their communities and congressional districts. It focuses specifically on this diverse organizational landscape and how groups have worked together and separately to channel the energy in the streets into work in local communities and congressional districts leading up to the 2018 midterm elections.

Chapter Three

ORGANIZING THE RESISTANCE
IN THE DISTRICTS

IN THE FALL OF 2018, I took the students in my graduate course in activism to Capitol Hill to observe the protests against Judge Kavanaugh's nomination to the Supreme Court. We met in the lobby of the Senate Hart Building, which was overwhelmed with hundreds of protesters the following day.[1] Groups had been employing the full spectrum of tactics that week—organizing inside *and* outside Senate offices in the Hart Building.

Participants were encouraged to wear black T-shirts, so I changed out of my lecturing clothes and into a black T-shirt that said "What Glass Ceiling" before heading downtown. We spent the first half of the afternoon walking the halls of the Senate, observing citizens who had come to express their opposition to the nomination by interacting with senators, their staff, and the Capitol Police.[2] Because we were a group of nine people walking the marble halls in black T-shirts, we stood out amid the suits and heels that are standard dress in the Senate. We went down to the entrance to the capitol subway, a small train that transports members from the Senate office complex to their chambers in the U.S. Capitol,[3] hoping to observe protesters interacting with senators and their staff as they got on and off the subway and walked the long hallway. This tactic was being encouraged by protest organizers because it was a good place to find members and their staff where they had no place to hide. As we neared the subway entrance, it was clear that the Capitol Police were aware of the tactic and prepared to discourage us. One policewoman with an earpiece and a bundle of plastic zip ties—common gear for restraining protesters—dangling next to her gun barked, "Move along, no stopping here."

The police made it so uncomfortable to stand by the subway that we didn't linger in the tunnel. Instead, my students decided to stop by their senators' offices and express their opinions about the nominee. Together, a nine of us visited the offices of the senators from Florida, Ohio, and North Carolina, picking up whatever the office offered as treats from each state along the way. We ended our tour of the Senate at Maryland Senator Van Hollen's office. Though we missed seeing the senator, we chatted with the receptionists about what they had majored in when they were students at the University of Maryland and the crazy week of occupations in the Senate while drinking Florida orange juice and snacking on bags of nuts from North Carolina.

At 6 p.m., we walked over to a vigil on the steps of the Supreme Court. The vigil had the look and feel of a mainstream protest: groups passed out Cancel Kavanaugh and #StopKavanaugh posters for everyone to hold, and speakers addressed the crowd. We heard from survivors of sexual assault and Democratic Senator Kirsten Gillibrand (who had taken over Hillary Clinton's seat when she became Barack Obama's secretary of state in 2009).

Through this fieldtrip to Capitol Hill, my students had learned about the toolbox of tactics employed by social movements and the ways organizations coordinate activism both inside and outside institutional politics. Experiencing the different types of Resistance taking place on Capitol Hill firsthand, however, and how institutional actors in the Senate and the Capitol Police responded, felt completely different. Throughout the remainder of the semester, my students referenced this experience and reflected on how they felt during different parts of the day. This first hand experience was invaluable as we discussed the activism and social movements literature to understand different perspectives on contentious politics in a dark seminar room on the University of Maryland's campus.

Since the Resistance began in January 2017, Resisters have been engaged in other civil and political activities beyond marching. Across all events and issues—from women's rights to gun control—protesters have reported remarkably high levels of civic engagement (see chapter 2). The finding that people participating in demonstrations are more politically engaged than the general population is not surprising. Many scholars have noted that individuals who participate in activism tend to be joiners.[4] They are, therefore, more civically engaged than the rest of the population by default. At the same time, participating in a protest has become much more common in recent years. In the 2014 General Social Survey, less than 10 percent of the population reported participating in a rally or a demonstration.[5] Four years later, in August 2018, the Pew Research Center found that 14 percent of registered voters had attended "a political rally, protest or campaign event in the past year."[6] Accounts of protest participation among the general U.S. population (which includes voters and nonvoters) was even higher, with one poll reporting that one in five Americans had participated in a protest or political rally since 2016.[7] This increase in protest participation is consistent with the expectations of Caren and colleagues, who found that changes in more confrontational forms of political action, such as protests, are "likely to happen suddenly during periods of political unrest."[8]

The actions of President Trump and his administration have fanned the flames of resistance, motivating participation in marches focused on issues that span the progressive spectrum. The majority of participants in the resistance in the streets reported deciding to participate without any connection to the groups organizing each event.[9] Rather, like the research that finds moral shocks are an effective tool for mobilizing strangers, most respondents turning out without ties to organizations reported that they had seen calls to march on social media and elsewhere.[10] Moral shocks can be an effective tool for mobilizing strangers to participate in a march or, potentially, a number of marches, without personal ties to groups that do the work of organizing, but it is difficult to sustain activism.[11] Given that so few people in the streets reported being members of the groups that worked together to organize these marches, the role of organizations in turning out participants for the resistance in the streets seems to have been limited.[12]

Moreover, in exploring who persisted in the Resistance, Lorien Jasny and I examined the role organizations played across all of these large-scale protests in repeatedly turning people out. We found that "neither organizational membership, nor coming to the events with members of an organization" were associated with higher levels of protest participation.[13] Hearing about the event from an organization did not explain differential levels of participation either. In short, across the numerous measures of the role organizations can play in facilitating participation in protest, none of these measures explained who was the most involved and turned out again and again.

Although organizations have not played a strong role in turning out participants to march in the streets or getting them to march again and again, civic groups (which include organizations that coordinate demonstrations) are the connective tissue of democracy; they facilitate long-term activism and engagement. In the words of Kenneth T. Andrews, "strong organizations make possible the sort of sustained participation that supports a protest's agenda for the long haul."[14] In this chapter, I look at how groups have been working with motivated individuals to channel their outrage and energy from the streets into action in congressional districts and communities around the country.

In chapter 2, I presented evidence collected through surveys and observations with individual participants in the resistance in the streets. In this chapter, I present findings from open-ended, semistructured interviews conducted with the representatives of organizations that are leading the resistance in the districts, along with observations of their work in the field.[15]

Interviews were initially conducted with leaders of a number of groups in the winter of 2018. In the weeks leading up to the midterm elections in October 2018, and directly after the stunning but unsuccessful efforts to stop Brett Kavanaugh's confirmation to the Supreme Court, follow-up interviews were conducted (see appendix for details on my methods). The majority of these groups were formed in direct response to the outcome of the 2016 election, and many of them referred to themselves as "resistance groups," so I also use this term.

This chapter is divided into four sections. First, I provide an overview of the organizational landscape, focusing on the major resistance groups that set their sights on coordinating resistance in communities and in congressional districts in the lead-up to the midterm elections. Second, I discuss how these efforts focused on the local level. Third, I describe how these groups employed distributed organizing to fill an infrastructural void they had identified in their communities and districts. Finally, I explore the ways these resistance groups are working together and discuss some of the challenges to an organizational landscape that includes such a broad and unlikely coalition of groups working together to oppose the Trump agenda.

WHO ARE RESISTANCE GROUPS?

The organizational landscape of the Resistance is densely populated by groups with overlapping missions and constituencies. Most of the resistance groups are newly formed. Perhaps the best known is Indivisible, which began with a guide but quickly transitioned into an organization:

> After the 26-page Indivisible Guide was put online as a Google doc in mid-December 2016, it quickly went viral . . . and Google's servers kept crashing, rendering it virtually useless. Created by a group of former congressional staffers, the guide, now a website, provides specific tactics for fighting against President Donald Trump's agenda by taking a page from the Tea Party's playbook.[16]

The authors of the guide promptly formed an organization called Indivisible and, by the end of 2017, Indivisible reported that more than five thousand local "Indivisible" groups had been created across the country.[17] In October 2018, I sat down with the group's co-executive director, Leah Greenberg, in their new office space. Over a cup of coffee, she told me about her background working for Congressman Tom Perriello of Virginia. She noted that Indivisible groups exist in "every state and every congressional district" in the United States.[18]

Indivisible is not the only resistance group with such an origin story. The Town Hall Project, which aims to make information about town hall meetings with elected officials available to the general public, was launched by electoral campaign veterans as a Google document in January 2017, a few weeks after Indivisible went public.[19] It partnered with the organizers of March For Our Lives in spring 2018 to hold "Town Hall for Our Lives" events with elected officials regarding the issue of gun control. The group held more than 150 events in districts around the country during the congressional recess in the spring of 2018.[20] Throughout the 2018 election cycle, the Town Hall Project kept track of the 150 members of Congress who had not held a single town hall meeting during that session of Congress, which began in January 2017.[21] It also encouraged every candidate for public office to take their Town Hall Pledge, which committed elected officials to hold at least four town hall meetings with constituents each year they were in office.[22]

Indivisible and the Town Hall Project were both started by people who had been working in politics (and were fans of Google documents), but other new resistance groups had different origins. Swing Left, which aimed to change the party in control of the House of Representatives by focusing on swing districts around the United States, explained their group this way:

> We weren't politicians or professional organizers. Swing Left was started by a group of individuals from diverse industries, including tech, media, finance, nonprofits, and art. We are citizens. And like many people, we'd been sitting on the sidelines for too long. We didn't have all the answers, but we knew it was time to channel our anger and despair in a positive direction.[23]

The founders were motivated to form this new resistance group by their moral outrage. Swing Left was the main coordinator of The Last Weekend, which my sister and I had participated in on the weekend before the 2018 election (see chapter 1). The effort channeled the energy of more than sixty groups into "a massive get-out-the-vote effort aimed at helping Democratic candidates during the last days of the 2018 midterm election."[24]

Other new resistance groups were created for different purposes but ended up redirecting their focus to the midterm elections. Recall that the Women's March was formed in response to a series of individual calls to action on Facebook. Bob Bland, the creator and co-chair of the Women's March, described to me her path to coleading the group when we met a week after Brett Kavanaugh was confirmed to a lifetime appointment on the Supreme Court. Bland came to our meeting directly from dealing with her arrest during the Kavanaugh protests. She recalled: "I didn't really get involved with either political or activism-related [work] for most of my adult life until two years ago." Telling me about her work in the fashion industry and how it led her to design and produce a "Nasty Woman" T-shirt after the third presidential debate in 2016, she explained: The T-shirt "went viral . . . by noon [the next day], I was selling one a second . . . and with that, came this whole community of nasty women who were suddenly engaging with me online and saying, 'What else can we do?'"[25]

After the 2017 Women's March, the national organization shifted its focus. Bland explained that the leaders of the group felt they needed to continue their work and follow through on the momentum of the Women's March.[26] The group coordinated numerous events, including the #Enough National School Walkout on March 14, 2017, and a series of protests during the Kavanaugh confirmation process, including one that overwhelmed the atrium of the Hart Building the day after my students and I had visited the Senate. Bland was arrested alongside actor-comedian Amy Schumer and many others.[27] In addition to these more confrontational tactics, the national group organized a tour to ten cities to focus on the midterm elections. It is notable that the group did not play a formal role in organizing the Women's March 2018, which mobilized an estimated two million people to demonstrate on the one-year anniversary of the first Women's march.[28]

In November of 2017, some of the leaders of the sister marches of the Women's March established their own group called March On.[29] By the beginning of 2018, both the National Women's March group and March On had redirected their efforts to the midterm elections. The groups ran separate but very similar campaigns: the National Women's March group's "Power to the Polls" and March On's "March On the Polls." Vanessa Wruble headed campaign operations for the National Women's March after working in media production. She left the group in 2017 and became executive director of March On. Wruble explained her group's decision to target the election: "We came to the conclusion that the only thing to do was to work on the midterms and all the other things we wanted to happen—reproductive rights, climate change, racial and social justice—there was just no real point in focusing on those things until we changed our representation. So that's how we ended up focusing on the elections."[30]

Along with these new groups, a number of more established organizations also focused their attention on the 2018 midterm elections. These established groups tend to be staffed by people with political backgrounds, including experience working for government agencies and organizing for progressive issues. In many cases, they are continuing previous projects and campaigns. One such example is the Hip Hop Caucus, which focuses on connecting the Hip Hop community to build power and create positive change. I spoke with the senior vice president of climate, environmental justice and community revitalization for the Hip Hop Caucus, Mustafa Santiago Ali, in the bright common room in his office right next to the group's sound studio. He told me about his decision to leave a career at the Environmental Protection Agency after twenty-three years to join the caucus, which was started in 2004. Then he described the purpose of the group's Respect My Vote campaign. It aims to get "more folks engaged in the civic process who might not normally be . . . [because they are] communities of color, young people, returning citizens."[31]

Another established group that invested in the midterm elections is MoveOn, which began as an email campaign to move beyond the efforts to impeach President Bill Clinton in 1998 and is a pioneer in the field of online organizing.[32] A focus in the districts around elections is not new to MoveOn, but this work expanded to be "more active in more districts" in 2018. Although MoveOn is not known for organizing big marches, it was involved in coalitions that have coordinated a number of demonstrations since the inauguration: it was an official partner of the 2017 Women's March, and it played a leadership role in organizing the Families Belong Together events in June 2018.[33]

In contrast to established groups that are continuing their pre-2016 efforts, the American Civil Liberties Union (ACLU) only began to focus on electoral work after the 2016 election. The group gained notoriety for the role it played in organizing a response to the Trump administration's efforts to implement its first travel ban in January 2017 (less than a week after the inauguration and the first Women's March). In collaboration with other groups, the ACLU mobilized thousands of lawyers to go to airports the weekend after the original executive order was signed.[34] In 2018, the ACLU began a new program, People Power, with the specific goal of engaging in electoral politics. The group's political director, Faiz Shakir, explained the motivation for starting People Power, which includes a fifty-state voting rights campaign:

> [In 2018], the ACLU plans to do electoral work in a serious way for the first time. We're getting involved in elections because the stakes are incredibly high for civil rights and civil liberties issues in America. The ACLU aims to educate voters about the civil liberties and civil rights records of candidates and build a base of voters who will factor those records into how they will vote. At the same time, we'll be mobilizing ACLU volunteers to ensure that Americans around the country understand the potential consequences of these elections.[35]

During all of these conversations, many organizers spoke about the connection between the resistance in the streets and the resistance in the districts leading up to the midterm elections. Perhaps Victoria Kaplan from MoveOn best summarized this point: "You can't just march and think that things are going to change. We march and we organize, and we vote."[36] Phil Aroneanu, the digital organizing strategy director at ACLU spoke about their members who are "interested in doing the kind of block-by-block work . . . that feels like it has meaningful outcomes. . . . It's not just about protesting every word that comes out of Trump's mouth. It's about building the kind of future that we want to see and protecting our communities." This seasoned organizer reflected on how his observations from people working with the ACLU compared with other groups: "I'm hearing that same assessment from friends at various other organizations as well. . . . A lot of the folks who joined those groups are also foot soldiers in electoral campaigns or in ballot measure campaigns, which is what we're seeing on our end as well."[37] Regardless of the original mission of these groups, a clear consensus emerged among resistance groups across the organizational landscape that they needed to focus their efforts in communities and in congressional districts leading up to the midterm elections in November 2018.

FROM THE BARRICADES TO THE BALLOTS IN CONGRESSIONAL DISTRICTS

The background and focus of resistance groups are somewhat diverse, but when asked what motivated them to become involved in resistance in the districts, a clear consensus was that they were driven to act as a direct response to the election of Donald Trump and the policies being promoted by the Trump administration.[38] To achieve their objective, most resistance groups stressed the need to invest in politics at the local level. For years, scholars have noted significant changes taking place in U.S. politics. Many have observed a growing disconnect between regular people and politics, and with the profession-alization of interest-oriented political organizations, members of civic groups have become more like consumers and less like engaged participants.[39]

In *Activism, Inc.*, I discussed how passive participation and armchair activism compares with campaigns that involve members in meaningful ways. By analyzing the campaign strategies and political infrastructure of the Right and the Left during the 2004 elections, I found substantial differences that had significant effects on how the grass roots in the districts were mobilized and engaged on both sides. The Republicans rallied local networks of conservatives to work for their campaigns in swing states, whereas the Democrats relied on paid professionals and imported volunteers from blue states to canvass and do their campaign work. In other words, the Democrats were laying sod while the Republicans were cultivating the grass.[40]

One unifying theme across all of the resistance groups was their recognition that the Left needed to address this weakness, investing in developing true grassroots connections with individuals at the local level. For example, the chief communications officer of Indivisible, Sarah Dohl, spoke specifically about how the group's focus is locally directed: "our theory of change is that the only voices that matter are the people within a congressional district . . . [it's like] a 50-state strategy without being top-down."[41] This member of the leadership team at Indivisible referenced the so-called 50-state strategy originally pushed by DNC chair Howard Dean after the 2004 election. The goal of this strategy was to build a Democratic grassroots infrastructure. It was resuscitated by DNC chair Tom Perez after the 2016 election and renamed "every zip code counts," but it attracted quite a bit of criticism.[42]

Mustafa Ali Santiago of the Hip Hop Caucus, which has been working in communities of color for fourteen years, also highlighted the importance of local infrastructure: "You see lots of organizations that often parachute into vulnerable communities and some are well meaning, but folks know they're only going to be there for a little while, not create authentic connections that take time and hardly ever make long-term investments that support communities in building their own capacity." Vanessa Wruble, the leader of March On, had a similar perspective: "It's against our ethos to parachute into a place and be like, 'we're going to set this up here because this is what's going to work.'"[43] These statements from 2018 echo a number of the critiques of the practices of Left-leaning groups and the Democratic Party in the early 2000s.

In the wake of the 2016 election, Democrats triumphed in both the special elections and the off-cycle 2017 elections.[44] Longtime organizer Phil Aroneanu, who works with the ACLU, acknowledged the importance of local efforts when reflecting on the post-2016 Democratic electoral victories: "The engine that drove a lot of those victories was really just people busting their butts at the local level—knocking on doors, raising money, posting on social media . . . the real action is happening locally."[45]

The importance of the local level of politics is also recognized by new groups that aim to support candidates in swing districts in Congress (Swing Left) and flippable seats in state elections (Flippable). Even though these groups pooled resources and recruited volunteers who, in many cases, did not live in the candidates' districts, the groups' leaders acknowledged that successful campaigns come from the local level. Ethan Todras-Whitehill, executive director and cofounder of Swing Left, explained how that group's work supports local interests: "We trust the Democrats in a district to pick the best candidate for themselves, and then we'll be there to support those nominees."[46] During 2018, numerous local resistance groups reported working with Swing Left on their specific campaigns.

The conviction that local people need to select their own candidates differs from Democratic Party practices in recent years.[47] For example, the Democratic Party backed incumbents Joe Crowley and Michael Capuano against their more progressive primary challengers Alexandra Ocasio-Cortez and Ayanna Pressley during the 2018 election (both women went on to win).[48] Although supporting incumbents on the ballot is not surprising, it was less expected that the Democratic Party would take sides when no Democratic incumbent was on the ballot. For example, in 2018, the Democratic Congressional Campaign Committee (DCCC) reportedly funded campaign ads against a progressive Democratic candidate running in the seventh congressional district in Texas.[49]

A number of resistance groups mentioned working on specific primary campaigns, which has been a standard tactic for Right-leaning groups since at least 2008. In fact, leaders of some resistance groups told me they had supported primary candidates who were not being supported by the Democratic Party.[50] Leah Greenberg of Indivisible explained: "Our position has always been that primaries are super healthy . . . one thing that sets our endorsement program apart is that it is not structured fundamentally around who has the best chance of getting elected." Greenberg went on to connect this practice to potential long-term political outcomes: "Somebody who loses their congressional race [in 2018] may run for state legislature, and they will have built their name identification and a volunteer network this year." She also highlighted ways that supporting candidates that local groups are excited about can be good for Democrats, and for democracy more generally. In some cases, Indivisible groups are "knocking on doors for congressional candidates whom they know, because the candidate has been coming to events [and] has been really actively engaged with the grassroots community in a way that the [up ticket] candidate is not."[51] Supporting local candidates who may not have a good chance of winning is a strategy for "contributing to up ticket enthusiasm," which has the potential to lead to broader positive electoral outcomes for Democrats.

HARNESSING DISTRIBUTED ORGANIZING TO OVERCOME THE CHALLENGES OF AN INFRASTRUCTURAL DEFICIT

This focus on local engagement and representation, along with groups reserving the right to challenge candidates in the

Democratic primaries, is part of a broader critique by members of the Resistance regarding the workings of the Democratic Party. In my previous work, I concluded that the Democratic Party was investing only in local contact that "ensures that the locals are contacted, but it does not engage the local institutions of civil society that have enduring roots in communities."[52] The lasting effects of this process are that the Democratic Party did not establish any infrastructure for the future. Indeed, hiring people to do voter outreach and grassroots mobilization, or importing them from blue states—"parachuting" them in as the leaders of the Hip Hop Caucus and March On mentioned instead of working directly with local groups and local volunteers—has had lasting effects.

During my conversations with leaders of resistance groups, the Democratic Party's infrastructural weaknesses were repeatedly acknowledged. Catherine Vaughan, founder of Flippable, explained that her group was focused on state-level races and noted that state politics "have been overlooked by Democrats for decades, despite being the key to electoral policies such as redistricting and voting rights."[53] This sentiment was echoed by most groups. Even leaders of groups that worked directly with the Democratic Party pointed out that local infrastructure has "never really been done by the Democratic Party in an effective way . . . [the Party] would be the logical place to do this, but again, that's not what they're set up to do. Really to do grassroots mobilization, you need to have something people can mobilize behind."[54]

Resistance groups have emerged to fill this perceived gap. The ACLU's Aroneanu explains: "People Power popped up post [2016] election to fill the . . . vacuum. . . . This is stuff that political parties could be doing, but they are not." Victoria Kaplan from MoveOn takes this point further by connecting this vacuum directly to the Democratic Party. She notes that many members' "interest in volunteering with an organization like MoveOn is because they don't see their Democratic Party anywhere." The founders of Indivisible also described how their efforts were focused on the kind of local work that its leaders recognized was missing and needed. In the words of the group's chief communications officer, Sarah Dohl, "Progressives and the Left have really lacked a ground game for a long time. We haven't had to have one . . . this concept of really getting people out at home and showing up at congressional district offices to lobby on issues like taxes, that's something the Democrats really have never had to do before."[55] Across all of these groups there was a clear consensus that the Democratic Party had failed to cultivate true grassroots engagement at the local level.

For a political infrastructure to support successful campaigns, groups on the Left must put in the time and effort and lay down roots where the party's base lives, works, and votes, mobilizing people locally and engaging them in a meaningful way.[56] Although the fifty-state strategy implemented by Howard Dean in 2005, as well as independent efforts by the 2008 Obama for America campaign, aimed to fill this infrastructural void, the consolidation of Organizing for America into the Democratic Party after the 2008 election cut off the roots of many of these efforts.[57] The Resistance is a direct response by progressive Americans to fill this infrastructural deficit; the focus of resistance groups on the local level is a clear response to these perceived weaknesses.

To capitalize on the energy of the Resistance, these groups have embraced a "distributed organizing" model to fill the infrastructural vacuum. Each organization and organizer had a somewhat different interpretation and implementation of distributed organizing. When asked to define what, exactly, this model entailed and how it was different from more traditional organizing models, the response was hazy. Victoria Kaplan explained that "we hear the term 'distributed organizing' a lot, and it's all in how you actually define it, because different people will define it differently." Another leader admitted: "To be honest, I don't even know what it means. I'm told it's 'distributed organizing,' so I use the words, but I haven't had the time to even think at that level."[58] Although most leaders of the Resistance had trouble defining this concept, their efforts to implement distributed organizing had three distinct characteristics: fluid membership, loosely affiliated networks, and geographically diffuse activism. All of these characteristics are facilitated by digital tools.

FLUID MEMBERSHIP

This new conception of membership builds directly on the innovative model used by MoveOn to reach out to members via email, invite them to participate in activities, and solicit donations. For all groups, membership is fluid and, instead of involving some sort of dues or service, is defined as those who show interest by signing up through an event or on a list.[59] As a result, people are members of numerous groups simultaneously and may have very limited connection to the group.

While writing this book, for example, I signed up for events sponsored by most of the resistance groups I was studying. Since then, I have been treated like a member: I receive all of their news and action alerts via email (and have been asked for donations repeatedly).

Leah Greenberg spoke directly about what membership means to local chapters that call themselves "Indivisible groups":

> Identity is often fluid for these groups . . . [one week they] will do a Planned Parenthood action, and the next week they'll be going to their local sanctuary city/town thing, and they'll be wearing their Women's March hats. . . . The independence and the many-flowers-bloom part of this is really important and a good thing. . . . We neither want nor expect that people are only doing . . . our priority campaigns.

Vanessa Wruble discussed March On's similar approach:

> You don't have to call yourself March On. . . . You can call yourself whatever you want. . . . We have Indivisible groups in our network and people who call themselves something new. . . . We're not about that.

This "many-flowers-bloom" phrase is from a well-known Maoist saying about the Communist Party of China welcoming differing perspectives.[60] Across the board these groups expressed no territorial sentiments about their members.

Despite the fluidity of membership, many groups spoke about the size of their lists as a measure of power. Others noted that it was not the size of the list but the "brand loyalty" based on "quality engagement" that determined the success of their efforts. Although the fluidity of membership was seen as a positive, it is likely that the shifting notion of membership may explain why so few participants in the resistance in the streets identified themselves as members of the groups that had organized the events. When membership is determined by "signing up" on a website or showing interest in an event, rather than by paying dues or going to a weekly meeting, members do not necessarily develop a strong identity or solidarity with the groups they are supposedly joining.

LOOSELY AFFILIATED NETWORKS

Resistance groups work through a nonfederated structure that connects to national groups as nodes in a network. Distributed organizing gives local groups much more autonomy and fewer formal pathways. Although local civic groups are known to be diverse, coming in all shapes and sizes, those that are connected with a national group have historically followed a federated model that mimics the political structure in the United States. This structure connects the local level to the state level and then to the federal level.[61] In her work on the *People's Lobby*, University of Chicago professor Elisabeth Clemens documents how interest groups in American history institutionalized specific patterns of political organization.[62]

Phil Aroneanu from the ACLU explained that groups using the distributed organizing model may have "highly localized organizing structures that are sometimes not coordinated very well at the national level."[63] In their behinds-the-scenes account of the distributed organizing work on the Sanders campaign in 2016, Bond and Exley highlighted how distributed organizing cultivates volunteer leaders in the absence of paid staff.[64] Organizations that follow such a participatory structure tend to be more democratic, but research has shown time and again how this structure makes decision making much more difficult.[65]

For the most part, resistance groups reported employing this bottom-up approach. In some cases, local groups were just small informal collectives of like-minded individuals who cared about any issue or many issues. Bob Bland describes the variation in the groups working with the National Women's March group: "some of them have no formal structure, some of them are just meetups where they only focus on certain events. Some of them have incorporated . . . it really depends on the size and . . . the will of the members." The co-executive director from Indivisible echoed this sentiment, reporting that local Indivisible group structure "just varies a lot based on the state, based on the leaders, based on who has the time in order to put in the work there."[66]

When I asked if Indivisible's national office helps to encourage and maintain a specific structure for their groups, Greenberg described a philosophy that clearly distinguishes their format from the federated structure of civic groups of the past. Early on, she explained, "we recognized that our core value as a national entity was going to be supporting the work of local groups on the ground, that really nothing mattered if there weren't empowered leaders around the country who were charting their own course and making change in their own communities. Our central role is to support that through a whole variety of different ways. . . . We think of ourselves as a large node within a network." As a large node, Indivisible provides numerous resources to local group leaders: "We can support your work organizing your group and coordinating with other Indivisibles; help you amplify what you're doing for the world to see; and offer resources and support systems for things like fundraising and insurance."[67] Resources included access to regional and state organizers who coordinate with those local groups that are interested, regional institutes that bring group leaders together, as well as webinars and local organizing guides.

GEOGRAPHICALLY DIFFUSE ACTIVISM

It is ironic that this very local work is not necessarily done by local people. Even though groups are mainly made up of loosely affiliated organizations and locally situated individuals, distributed organizing makes it possible for resistance groups to harness the power of interested individuals from all over the country. Organizing is no longer coordinated through brick-and-mortar offices geographically situated in the communities where members work, so distributed organizing need not mobilize people to take action in the communities in which they live. Rather, it enables groups to capitalize on the energy they draw from members who may not be located in any particular geographic location. As the digital organizing strategy director of the ACLU put it, geographically diffuse activism "helps us to redistribute capacity to the places that need it most." Aroneanu provided examples of working with ACLU members in New York and California on campaigns in other parts of the country. However, he also stressed that the group was working to capitalize on the actual location of their members whenever possible:

> We try to tap into People Power networks to create a sense of community and a sense that if, for example, you're in West Virginia, you should be spending your time working on West Virginia. [But] we're not going to force somebody to engage on an issue or tactic that they are not interested in. If you live in West Virginia but you really want to call into Michigan on a voting rights measure, knock yourself out.[68]

During the 2018 election cycle, resistance groups employed distributed organizing to capitalize on the power of progressive Americans around the country. Swing Left laid out a clear strategy on their website for integrating the energy and resources of people no matter where they lived:

> We all want to take back the House in 2018, but most of us don't live in Swing Districts, where the races really matter. If you live . . . (1) **Outside this district**, you'll receive opportunities to help from afar; (2) **Near this district** (or it's easy for you to travel), you can decide to help out in person; (3) **Inside this district**, your support and knowledge are critical! Join your team and help channel its efforts.[69]

By capitalizing on interested people from all over and giving *near locals* opportunities for face-to-face activities, distributed organizing techniques enabled resistance groups to take advantage of the energy of movement sympathizers no matter where they lived.

The specific efforts described by organizers, as well as distributed organizing more generally, is only possible due to digital technologies. In the 2018 election, technology made it possible for candidates to raise "record-shattering amounts of small-donor cash" and mobilize "unprecedented armies of volunteers."[70] For example, when my sister and I volunteered in Virginia's tenth district, we signed up through a link provided in an email I received from Indivisible that directed us to The Last Weekend website, which was coordinated by Swing Left. The website gave us a list of the closest swing districts and activities taking place where we could volunteer in person.

Beyond The Last Weekend, resistance groups all mentioned making resources digitally available for individual members and local groups. Perhaps the best known resources are from Indivisible, which made its name by releasing a guide in December 2016 and has since made many other digital tools available for its groups. But they were not alone. Victoria Kaplan from MoveOn told me that "we put together materials, sort of like a *campaign-in-a-box*, so that even if you haven't been to a MoveOn member summit or joined a training call, you could organize and host an event, because we provided all the tools and materials for you." Many other resistance groups reported providing such resources for events, including the ACLU, which made available "guides and different kinds of resources and various touch points."[71]

Resources were shared through a digital repository like a Google drive, and online resources facilitated communication among groups and members through technologies like Slack, and to the general public through various social media platforms. All of these digital tools made it possible for people to participate from around the country. In some cases, people took on the role of a "phone bank host in their living room for three or four weeks leading up to the election." Although most groups provided opportunities for people to do their activism wherever they wanted whenever they were available, most groups also provided opportunities to channel motivated individuals into live, face-to-face interactions, meetings, and opportunities. Aroneanu told me about how the ACLU had merged their traditional field organizing program, which is run out of physical buildings in the states, with the distributed program they had built through People Power. He reflected that it "gave us the opportunity to leverage the benefits of both having a distributed network of volunteers and having a set of staff to help organizing offices around the country."[72]

During the 2018 campaign, MoveOn took advantage of distributed organizing and digital tools to amplify their members' efforts to support political campaigns through what they called "Wave Events." The group's organizing director explains:

> I post the details of my event, I let my friends, and my fellow Resisters, and neighbors and people I've been organizing with, and going to marches with, . . . I let them know they're invited . . . MoveOn also emails and sends text messages to MoveOn members near me in my congressional district.

I've got some MoveOn Resist & Win buttons and T-shirts to hand out: we've got some signs. While the candidate's in the office, she'll take a picture with us, she posts it on Twitter saying, "Thanks, MoveOn members for coming and helping to get out the vote." . . . We go out, we knock on doors. Instead of just me having conversations with eight or ten voters during my shift, I've multiplied my impact because there are thirty-five of us who are out there doing that.[73]

These wave events were made possible through distributed organizing using digital tools. An individual makes the first move, but instead of the individual being fully responsible for organizing the event through a local civic group or her friends and neighbors, members are mobilized using algorithms that identify who on the voluminous MoveOn list lives in the area and might be willing to participate. Participants are then prepared for the event through digital resources from the campaign-in-a-box, making it possible for strangers to come together at an event that highlights the MoveOn brand. The event is amplified through social media.

SUSTAINING AN UNLIKELY COALITION

Most resistance groups reported connections to one another, and these connections have taken various forms. The chief communications officer of Indivisible noted that many of their local groups were formed on buses coming home from the Women's March in January 2017. When asked about working with other resistance groups, most leaders spoke about collaborations and numerous campaigns working with groups in their communities. More established organizations also connected with resistance groups. For example, during the March For Our Lives, the Hip Hop Caucus's "Respect My Vote" campaign capitalized on the event by sending an "army of hundreds of volunteers to register young voters."[74] The campaign reported registering more than fifteen hundred people who were marching in the streets so they could vote in their districts, which spanned forty different states.

Swing Left also reported working with many groups. When asked how they connect with other resistance groups, Todras-Whitehill pointed out that they "work with some Indivisible groups as closely as [with] some groups that call themselves Swing Left. We consider ourselves a conduit for the larger activism ecosystem, a way for anyone to do electoral work in these key House races."[75]

Conceived in the summer of 2018, Swing Left was the main organizer for The Last Weekend, but it was supported by more than sixty organizations that ran the gamut from general political groups to issue-specific groups. These groups included Indivisible, March On, MoveOn, and Flippable, as well as Climate Hawks Vote, Working Families, and the National Domestic Workers Alliance. As a "member" of many of these groups, I received numerous direct emails from them appealing to my interest in "doing more" and requesting that I sign up to volunteer through their group's on-ramp into The Last Weekend website.

The appeal worked, and my sister and I became near locals canvassing in Virginia's tenth district the weekend before the midterm elections (see chapter 1). This effort harnessed the energy of the Resistance by taking advantage of distributed organizing, and it focused on turning out droves of volunteers, most of whom were nonlocals who did not know one another or any people in the communities where they were volunteering to do voter contact before the election. At the end of the weekend, I received a bulk email reporting how our efforts did in the tenth district of Virginia and suggesting other ways we could stay involved. However, after five hours of volunteering, I had made no personal connections to anyone who lived or worked in the district beyond some short conversations at the door. Moreover, I had no personal connections to people who were interested in working for progressive change in this congressional district or community. The Last Weekend was a digitally enabled machine that channeled the energy and enthusiasm of Democratic voters to the places where it was needed. But for all the hype and connection to resistance groups that had been tirelessly working to connect local people together to work in their communities and make social change, it neither built local infrastructure nor developed local capacity within specific organizational networks or communities. Once again, the Left was relying on an instrumental structure that treated interested progressives as cogs in a political machine, this time parachuting in nonlocals to turn out voters instead of connecting local people through meaningful engagement.[76]

Numerous accounts of tensions emerged among leaders of the resistance groups. For example, different leadership styles were highlighted in the *New York Times* just before the first anniversary of the Women's March. The article focused on tensions between the organizers of the National Women's March group and those who coordinated sister marches in 2017 and went on to work together as the new group March On. The article discussed the national group's concerns about the branding of the Women's March. This topic gained increasing attention at the end of 2018. Vanessa Wruble from March On told me that the Women's March "talked about organizing horizontally and all that, but ultimately, it ended up being enormously top-down."[77] In many ways, this dispute highlights common tensions that have been found to exist between organizations with different leadership styles and philosophies, as well as among more informal local groups and the more professionalized national groups, even when they focus on the same progressive issue.[78]

With so many new organizations working in the districts leading up to the midterm elections, it is not a surprise that tension developed among the diverse groups and issue areas that make up the broad countermovement of the Resistance. Even though leaders of most of the resistance groups explicitly mentioned working together at some point during our conversations, interorganizational friction was bound to emerge. Organizing for the long term is hard; it requires a consistent flow of human and financial resources, both of which are finite. As a result, some level of competition among these groups is inevitable. As time goes on, resistance groups with different philosophies, different issue areas and priorities, and different perspectives on how to achieve their goals are likely to clash over their positions and tactics. Such conflicts are extremely common among political coalitions.[79]

With an organizational landscape that is densely populated with overlapping interests, constituencies, and funding streams, maintaining this unlikely coalition will be fraught with the possibility of conflicts and competition. And the potential of conflict will only grow as the stakes get higher and groups turn their attention to specific policy priorities, as well as the herculean task of selecting a Democratic nominee to run against Donald Trump in 2020.

SUMMARY

This chapter describes how groups have been focusing their efforts to channel the energy and enthusiasm from the resistance in the streets to resistance in the districts. Employing the benefits of distributed organizing, resistance groups have worked tirelessly to encourage engagement and focus on local issues while simultaneously building a system for harnessing energy from outside specific areas. Distributed organizing makes geographically diffuse activism possible, but there is no evidence that this strategy will create any lasting infrastructure in communities beyond the 2018 election. In chapter 4, I present the findings of follow-up surveys with those who marched in the streets to assess the success of these efforts to mobilize people to work on the midterm elections. In particular, I look at the ways participants of the resistance in the streets channeled their energy into work in their communities and congressional districts during the 2018 election cycle.

Chapter Four

RESISTANCE IN THE DISTRICTS

IN JULY 2018, I gave a keynote address at the March for Science summit in Chicago. The aim of the summit was "turning a March into a Movement."[1] The summit was filled with discussions of science advocacy, science communication, and community organizing, but the opening remarks began with a reminder from the organizers about the upcoming midterm elections. Stressing the importance of participating in the political system, one of the organizers began the meeting by encouraging everyone in the audience to register to vote. She directed them to an app designed specifically to register conference participants to vote with the hashtag #VoteForScience. The app connected to a website that explains: "Vote for Science is the next step for science advocacy: securing the long-term future of science policy by linking science support with civic behavior. It's time to create a direct connection between science supporters and our policymakers to strengthen science's voice in policy and politics."[2]

By beginning this conference on science activism with a nonpartisan plug for engaging in electoral politics, organizers of the March for Science were following the pattern of organizers of the Women's March and numerous other resistance groups (see chapter 3). Across all the groups that have organized marches since Donald Trump's inauguration in January 2017, there has been an increasing focus on electoral politics generally and on the midterm elections in particular. This glimpse into the meeting of the organizers of one of the large marches in the Resistance provides even more evidence that the Resistance has become a site of interaction between social movements and electoral politics. Doug McAdam and Karina Kloos remind us that "in truth, most movements have no interest in engaging with parties or national politics more generally."[3] However, some more recent research highlights the ways movements have connected with electoral politics, focusing on the post-9/11 antiwar movement and the Tea Party.[4] The Resistance provides a clear contemporary example of how this countermovement has moved from the streets into the districts to focus its efforts on electoral politics.

Chapter 3 documents how resistance groups worked to channel the energy and outrage of participants in the resistance in the streets into work in their communities and in targeted congressional districts around the country. In this chapter, I look at what participants in the resistance in the streets did in the lead-up to the midterm elections and the ways they worked with resistance groups. We know that people who participated in the resistance in the streets marched for a range of progressive issues (see chapter 2), from women's rights to gun control to immigration rights and beyond.[5] Across all events and issues, Resisters have reported doing much more than just marching in the streets, so it is not unexpected that they would also work in their communities for electoral change. The questions that remain are: What did Resisters do leading up to the midterm elections? and To what degree did Resisters work with resistance groups?

To answer these questions, I present the findings from two waves of follow-up surveys from participants originally surveyed during resistance in the streets events: the first administered six months before the midterm elections in May 2018, and the second administered two days after the midterm elections in November 2018 (for details, see the appendix). I look at how these participants in the Resistance worked with organizations to affect social change, which groups they worked with, what they identify as the top issues facing our country, and how they believe these problems can be solved. In contrast to the survey responses presented in chapter 2, the follow-up surveys included open-ended questions, which enables me to provide details about the experiences of Resisters in their own voices (all names are pseudonyms).

WORKING WITH GROUPS THAT ARE ORGANIZING THE RESISTANCE

When I asked participants of the resistance in the streets at each demonstration if they were connected with any of the groups sponsoring the march, most said no. Instead, a majority of participants in the resistance in the streets reported deciding to participate without any connection to the groups that organized or sponsored the event; they reported neither hearing about the event from a group nor traveling to the event with a group (see chapter 3). With the exception of the People's Climate March—the second large-scale mobilization of the climate movement in the United States in three years[6]—the marches in the Resistance were not directly connected to specific groups or campaigns that existed before the election of Donald Trump.

Many of the protest events I surveyed were originally called for by concerned individuals via social media, and these people were not directly connected to organizations doing work on the issue.[7] Most protest participants did not report hearing about the different marches from an organization (the average across events was 20 percent) and only slightly more protest participants reported being a member of a group that was part of the organizing coalition sponsoring each event (the average across events was 21 percent).

Table 4.1 presents the responses by participants at each protest to questions regarding their ties to sponsoring organizations. These numbers are particularly remarkable because the research on social movements and protests has found that organizations play a significant role in mobilizing protest participants. In an analysis of data collected from the American Civic Participation Study in 1989, Alan Schussman and Sarah Soule concluded that "the process of generating protest participation begins long before the appeal or invitation in organizations."[8] In my earlier study of five protest events around the issue of

TABLE 4.1 Marchers' connection to sponsoring organization (in percent)

	Women's March 2017	March for Science	People's Climate March	March for Racial Justice	Women's March 2018	March For Our Lives	Families Belong Together
Heard about march from organization	13	14	38	22	20	15	32
Member of organization in event coalition	18	20	37	16	17	16	24

Source: Author's own data.

globalization from 2000 to 2002, which is called "How Do Organizations Matter," I asked participants the same questions about their connections to organizations. I found that 41 percent of protest participants had heard about the events from organizations.[9] More recently, in a study of sixty-nine street demonstrations in seven countries in Europe, 49 percent of participants were members of one or more organization that was involved in staging the demonstration.[10]

The lower rates of organizational embeddedness (the connections to organizations that are working as a coalition to coordinate each event)[11] at these protest events can be explained, in part, by the events originally being called for by concerned individuals via social media. Another factor related to these low percentages is how membership in groups has changed with the advent of distributed organizing. As membership has become more fluid and is no longer determined by attending meetings or paying dues, individuals have only a tenuous connection to the groups that claim them as members. It is quite possible that many participants in the resistance in the streets were members of the groups that were in the organizing coalition, but they didn't even realize it. This interpretation is consistent with David Karpf's findings in his study of MoveOn as it transitioned from "forgettable 1998 startup to left-wing juggernaut." Karpf stated that group " 'members' often don't even know that they are members; they just know that they receive a lot of e-mails from the organization."[12]

With the fluidity of membership in this era of distributed organizing, many protest participants may have responded negatively to a question on a survey during a demonstration in the streets of Washington, D.C. that asked "Are you a member of any organization or group that was involved in organizing this protest?"—even though groups in the organizing coalition had these Resisters on their email and/or membership lists. Moreover, because one of the main elements of membership in this era of distributed organizing is receiving email, members may not even recognize that they heard about an event from a specific group when it comes in as part of a flood of email.

To understand better the effects of the limited role organizations played in the resistance in the streets despite the documented importance of civic groups and other types of organizations in channeling interested people into political work,[13] both waves of my follow-up survey specifically asked participants to discuss how they worked with organizations in their communities and in congressional districts after marching in the streets. The organizations named on the follow-up surveys were the same groups that were interviewed in chapter 3. Across every group, participation rates reported in November were much higher than the rates reported by Resisters six months before the election in May. A little over half (55 percent) of the Resisters responding to the first follow-up survey (May 2018) reported working in some capacity with groups listed on the survey. In the second survey (November 2018), two days after the midterm elections, an overwhelming majority of Resisters (81 percent) reported that they had worked with at least one of the groups listed on the survey in the lead-up to the midterm elections.[14] The group most Resisters reported "participating in activities/working with" in the November 2018 follow-up survey was the Democratic Party (60 percent). More than a quarter of participants also reported working with a number of resistance groups, including the National Women's March group (44 percent), MoveOn (36 percent), Indivisible (30 percent), and the ACLU (28 percent) during the lead-up to the election. Table 4.2 lists the groups most often mentioned by Resisters in each wave of the follow-up surveys.

The follow-up surveys also asked what work respondents did with organizations. The surveys listed activities that represent common types of volunteer political work (respondents could choose as many options as appropriate): attending a meeting, donating money, participating in a lobby event, participating

TABLE 4.2 Groups Resisters worked with after marching (in percent)

Since the inauguration, have you participated in activities/worked with . . .	May 2018	November 2018
Democratic Party	38	60
Women's March*	21	44
MoveOn	21	36
Indivisible	19	30
ACLU/People Power	14	28
Swing Left	8	18
March On	6	15

*Due to issues that arose regarding who had the right to use the name "Women's March," it is possible that respondents were unsure which of the two women's march groups they should select.

Source: Author's own data.

in a sponsored canvass, participating in a town hall meeting, participating in a voter registration drive, signing a petition, or other (write in another activity). With so many groups focusing their efforts on the midterm elections, the ways individuals participated ran the gamut. Table 4.3 shows the activities Resisters participated in with these organizations.

"Mail-in membership" and "check-book activism" have been the focus of much political and civic participation in recent years,[15] so it may not be a surprise that donating money was the most common way respondents reported working with these groups. Over half of all participants in the follow-up survey in November (55 percent) reported giving money to at least one organization. But Resisters also engaged in many other activities.

TABLE 4.3 What respondents did with these groups (in percent)

In your work with the____, have you (check all that apply) . . .	May 2018	November 2018
Attended a meeting	26	37
Donated money	35	55
Participated in a lobbing event	11	21
Participated in a sponsored canvass	11	28
Participated in a town hall	13	17
Participated in a voter registration drive	9	19
Signed a petition	41	52

Source: Author's own data.

The second most common way people got involved in various groups was by signing a petition. About half (52 percent) of respondents reported signing petitions as part of their work with specific groups. This finding is consistent with the research by Caren and colleagues who noted a "robust increase" in the levels of petition signing in the United States between the 1970s and 2008 and interpreted this increase as being "promising for non-electoral forms of participation."[16] Leaders of resistance groups told me that petitions have become a common way for organizations with informal networks of members to gauge the preferences of their members. Petitions are used as an internal tool for organizations, rather than as a tactic for affecting broader social or political change. With most resistance groups focusing attention on the midterm election, this finding suggests that petitions have become a common form of electoral participation as well.

The third most popular activity was attending a meeting; more than one-third of all respondents (37 percent) reported attending the meeting of at least one of the groups listed on the survey. Just as participation in all groups went up during the six months prior to the midterm elections, participation in every type of activity that individuals could do with these groups also increased over this time period. In short, participants in the Resistance were working with groups more and doing more activities with them overall the closer it was to the midterm elections.

Substantial differences were found in how Resisters participated through these groups (see table 4.4). Signing a petition was a frequent activity for participants working with MoveOn (72 percent), March On (61 percent), Indivisible (60 percent),

TABLE 4.4 What respondents did, and with which group, November 2018 survey (in percent)*

In your work with the ___, did you . . .	Democratic Party N = 113	ACLU/ People Power N = 51	Indivisible N = 55	March On N = 28	MoveOn N = 65	Swing Left N = 32	Women's March N = 81
Attend a meeting	36	45	55	14	18	22	23
Donate money	69	73	38	32	42	41	38
Participate in a lobbying event	14	8	27	14	29	13	17
Participate in a sponsored canvass	43	8	25	11	9	22	4
Participate in a town hall meeting	19	8	20	4	5	3	6
Participate in a voter registration drive	28	12	16	7	11	9	4
Sign a petition	50	55	60	61	72	28	51

*Groups that engaged at least 15 percent of respondents; respondents could check more than one option.

Source: Author's own data.

the ACLU (55 percent), and the National Women's March group (51 percent). MoveOn, which rose to prominence during the public debate over efforts to impeach President Clinton in 1998, has long employed petitioning as a tool for gauging the interests of its members. Since the late 1990s, MoveOn has used petitioning to take the temperature of a fluid membership of supporters who do not necessarily attend meetings or interact face to face at all. In addition to signing petitions, 42 percent of the people who reported working with MoveOn donated money to the group, and 29 percent reported participating in a lobbying event with the group since the inauguration of Donald Trump in January 2017. Similarly, most people who reported working with the National Women's March group, which rose to prominence by organizing the largest march in U.S. history,[17] participated by signing a petition (51 percent). Resisters who reported working with this group also donated money (38 percent) and attended a meeting (23 percent).

Many Resisters worked with Indivisible, the group founded by former congressional staffers who released the *Indivisible Guide* in December 2016. Like MoveOn and the National Women's March group, signing a petition was the way most people participated with Indivisible. Respondents reported participating in the broadest range of activities with this group: 55 percent of the people who worked with Indivisible reported having attended a meeting with an Indivisible group, 38 percent reported giving them money, 27 percent reported participating in a lobby event, 25 percent reported participating in a sponsored canvass, and 20 percent reported attending a town hall meeting with the group.

More than one-quarter of participants in the follow-up survey also reported working with the ACLU/People Power: 73 percent donated money, 55 percent reported signing a petition, and 45 percent reported attending a meeting.

The Democratic Party had the largest number of Resisters working with it: 38 percent of all participants in the May 2018 follow-up survey reported participating in activities or working with the Democratic Party, and 60 percent of all participants reported working with the party in the November follow-up survey. Of the people who worked with the Democratic Party in the lead-up to the midterm elections, 69 percent reported donating money, 50 percent reported signing a petition, 43 percent participated in a sponsored canvass, and 36 percent reported attending a meeting. The Democratic Party is a political party, not a resistance group, and has a unique position among the groups I studied, so I asked additional questions about what Resisters may have done working with the party as part of the 2018 electoral cycle. In the lead-up to the midterm elections, 52 percent reported volunteering with a party-run campaign, 32 percent reported interacting with the national party in some way, and 16 percent reported seeking election for a local Democratic committee.

I also asked respondents to describe what work they did with individual candidate's campaigns (see table 4.5). About half of Resisters (52 percent) reported working with an individual candidate's campaign in November. Once again, most (67 percent) donated money, 49 percent of Resisters reported participating in a sponsored canvass, and 33 percent reported participating in a phone bank for a candidate. In addition, 31 percent of participants reported writing postcards in support of individual candidates. This finding is consistent with claims that this old-school tactic had once again become popular. In the words of *Washington Post* writer William Wan in the week of the midterm elections: "for tens of thousands of resistance-minded liberals in the age of Trump, the humble postcard has become a weapon of choice."[18]

I also asked respondents to write in the names of other groups they were working with in May and November of 2018. A third of all participants in the November follow-up survey, which was conducted two days after the election, wrote in at least one group beyond those listed on the survey. The most common write-in was a local Democratic committee, such as the "Democratic Club at Riderwood Village." No one wrote the name of the same group, but local Democratic groups represented 10 percent of all write-ins. The second most common

TABLE 4.5 What respondents did with individual candidate's campaigns

In your work with individual candidates, did you . . .	Percent
Donate money	67
Fund raise	10
Participate in a sponsored canvass	49
Phone bank	33
Recruit volunteers	14
Write postcards	31

Source: Author's own data.

type of write-in was hyperlocal community groups, such as "Liberal Woman of Chesterfield County" or "Organize Just Peace in Storrs Congregational Church." These groups represented 9 percent of all write-ins. In addition to the national groups that had been identified as working on progressive issues, many Resisters were also working with the Democratic Party, individual campaigns, and hyperlocal groups. This finding supports the claim by Putnam and Skocpol that the "Democratic Party, long in retreat, is being rebuilt."[19] Consistent with the local focus described by many resistance groups in chapter 3, Resisters reported working with the Democratic Party in ways that are locally embedded, locally focused, and directly linked with specific campaigns.

There were no overlaps in the most popular groups written-in to the surveys in May and November, and the *type* of groups that were the most popular in November were very different from those mentioned in the May follow-up survey. Six months before the midterm elections, most write-ins were issue-based groups working on the environment, gun control, and reproductive health. In the November survey directly following the election, most write-ins were political groups that tend to espouse more socialist perspectives on equity and the redistribution of wealth in America. Three groups tied for the most write-ins (each mentioned by four people, representing 6 percent of all mentions): the Democratic Socialists of America; the Poor People's Campaign; and Vote Forward, a group that encourages unlikely voters by sending personalized letters to them.[20]

Resisters participated in numerous activities and collaborations with resistance groups and campaigns leading up to the midterm elections in 2018. These people are not just donating money, they are participating in activities in their communities and congressional districts. This finding is in stark contrast to well-known critiques of American democracy that have found American civic life to be less directly connected to local efforts and more focused on "mail-in membership."[21] As students of democracy might hope, the percentage of Resisters participating in organizations around the country and the types of activities they engaged in with these groups grew substantially as the election approached.

THE TOP THREE ISSUES FACING AMERICA

Participants in the resistance in the streets were motivated to march by diverse and sometimes intersectional motivations that are identity-based and cross race, class, gender, sexual orientation, legal status, and other categories (see chapter 2).[22] To get a better sense of what Resisters believed to be the priority issues facing the country, both waves of the follow-up survey asked respondents to answer the question, "What are the top three issues facing our nation today?" Respondents provided 1,117 answers to this question over the two waves of the survey (not everyone provided three answers). These data were manually coded into categories. The top fifteen categories are shown in table 4.6. Like the diverse motivations that initially brought people out to participate in the various marches, opinions about the top issues spanned the full range of progressive issues. At the same time, there was some clear consensus among Resisters regarding the top issues facing America.

TABLE 4.6 Top issues facing the United States

	May 2018	Percent of responses	November 2018	Percent of responses
1	Environment	17	Environment	17
2	Civil rights	15	Political system	12
3	Political system	11	Health care	11
4	Welfare	10	Civil rights	10
5	Guns	6	Equality	9
6	Health care	6	Immigration	7
7	Gender	5	Guns	6
8	Immigration	4	Trump	5
9	Trump	3	Economy	4
10	Education	3	Racial justice	3
11	Equality	3	Women's rights	3
12	Economy	2	Welfare	3
13	Criminal justice	2	Education	2
14	Foreign policy	2	Foreign policy/reputation	2
15	Alt-facts/science	2	Facts	1

Source: Author's own data.

The environment, which included numerous mentions of climate change and rollbacks of environmental policies since the Trump administration took office, received the most mentions by far in both May and November. It received 17 percent of all mentions during each wave of the survey, and it was the most frequent choice for both the number one and number two issues in November 2018 after the midterms. Its importance to Resisters is particularly notable because the environment was the main focus of only one of the marches: the People's Climate March (although the March for Science also turned out people who were highly motivated by environmental issues).

The second most mentioned issue in November 2018 and the third highest in May was the political system. The variety of critiques about the U.S. political system included issues of dark money in politics, gerrymandering, and voter suppression. The political system received 12 percent of all mentions in November and 11 percent of all mentions six months earlier in May. This issue is distinct from specific mentions of President Trump and his presidency, which was given its own category and ranked ninth in May and eighth in November.

Health care was the third most mentioned issue in November, receiving 11 percent of all mentions. It rose from the sixth position in May when it had only 6 percent of all mentions. Attention to this issue is likely due, in part, to Republicans' continued efforts to dismantle the Affordable Care Act. The 115th Congress failed to repeal the Affordable Care Act during the first two years of the Trump presidency, but some states began to enforce work requirements for eligibility, and challenges to these state policies continue to work their way through the courts.[23]

Civil rights earned 10 percent of all mentions in November, which was 5 percent fewer than it earned six months earlier in May. Consequently, it dropped from the number two issue to the number four issue in November. This issue included mentions of bigotry, racism, concerns about white supremacy, and xenophobia. Specific mentions of racial justice, Black Lives Matter, or police brutality of nonwhites were coded as "racial justice" and ranked number ten in November, earning 3 percent of all mentions.

Priorities of participants in the Resistance were often similar to those of the voting public. Six weeks before the midterm elections, the Pew Research Center released the findings from a September 2018 survey of likely voters.[24] The Pew survey asked respondents what issues were "very important to their vote in 2018." The questions were not identical to those on my surveys, the respondents were "primed" to answer differently,[25] and the samples were different—registered voters versus participants in the resistance in the streets—but there were significant overlaps in the results. In fact, six of the top ten issues on the Pew survey also fell within the top ten issues on my follow-up surveys with Resisters: health care, the economy, guns, immigration, civil rights, and the environment.[26] These similarities are even more interesting because respondents in my follow-up surveys wrote in their responses, which were subsequently coded into categories. Although they could have offered whatever issue they wanted, the top issues voluntarily offered by Resisters overlapped substantially with the options listed on this telephone survey of a national sample of likely voters.

The top issue for these likely voters, who were surveyed by Pew during the confirmation process for Judge Brett Kavanaugh, was Supreme Court appointments. My November survey of Resisters was a few weeks after Judge Kavanaugh had been confirmed and the election had passed. At that time, the political system received a lot of attention, but not one participant in my postelection survey specifically mentioned the Supreme Court in their list of top issues, even when they discussed problems with the political system in America.

THE TOP SOLUTIONS GO LEFT

Across both waves of the follow-up survey, Resisters provided solutions for what they considered to be the top issues facing the United States. There were substantial differences between the solutions offered in May and November 2018.

BEFORE THE MIDTERMS

Six months before the midterm elections, there was clear consensus about how to solve the top issues facing America: no matter the issue, respondents overwhelmingly offered solutions that targeted institutional politics and specific changes from *inside* the political system. Of all the institutional political solutions, voting, the electoral process, and the midterm elections were mentioned the most. Respondents wrote in solutions that specifically addressed the electoral system and the need for citizens to participate in the 2018 midterm elections. Frequently, these political solutions were offered to solve issues identified with the U.S. political system. However, political solutions were also offered for other top issues mentioned by respondents. Many people mentioned changing the majority of the House of Representatives and the Senate from Republican rule, with a number of responses explicitly stating the need to "Elect Democrats" and "Flip the House of Representatives." Others just wrote in the term that had become popular as a reference to the Democratic Party gaining the majority in the Congress: "blue wave." Together these solutions represented 10 percent of all the responses to this question.

Political solutions did not focus only on the U.S. Congress and the election. Many Resisters also noted the need for a different administration. In fact, of the 602 individual solutions to the issues raised by respondents in May 2018, 3 percent specifically stated that the main avenue for addressing the top issues facing the United States was through the impeachment of President Trump. This solution was offered by some individuals surveyed at every single march in the Resistance.

In addition to focusing on the election and the administration, twelve political solutions (2 percent) referenced legislative options. Other solutions stressed the need to get dark money out of politics, with five solutions explicitly referencing the *Citizens United* decision handed down in January 2010—exactly seven years before the first Women's March flooded the streets of cities and towns across the United States with demonstrators the day after the inauguration of Donald Trump.[27] A small number of solutions called for more outsider political tactics, such as protest, activism, and the elimination of capitalism, but these less institutional solutions were a minority of all of the perspectives shared.

Solutions to environmental problems—considered to be the top issue facing America—covered a wide range of political options. Again, the focus was on institutional political solutions. Many people specifically stated that President Trump and his administration should be replaced, with a number of references to then administrator of the Environmental Protection Agency Scott Pruitt who stepped down in early July 2018 amid numerous ethics inquiries.[28] As Elizabeth, a twenty-seven-year-old woman from Washington County, Pennsylvania, originally surveyed at the People's Climate March in April 2017, put it, "Get Trump out of office, get Pruitt out of EPA, and keep pace with the rest of the world (ideally, we would lead) on sustainable energy."

Environmental issues were not only listed by participants surveyed at the People's Climate March and the March for Science, where the environment was the top motivation for attending the event, but these issues were of concern to people who had marched at the other events as well. In the words of Jenny, a fifty-year-old woman from Alexandria, Virginia, surveyed at the Women's March in 2018, solving environmental problems involved "ending subsidies for fossil fuels, increased investment in renewables, [and] stricter protections for the wilderness that is left." Many Resisters offered solutions to environmental issues that involved clear political options that focused on energy use, clean energy, and ways to address climate change. Numerous references also included the need for the United States to rejoin the Paris Agreement, which Donald Trump pulled out of in June 2017.[29]

In contrast to the various political avenues offered for solving environmental problems, most of the solutions mentioned to address civil rights, the number two issue in the May survey, focused explicitly on electoral politics. For example, Florence, a seventy-six-year-old white woman from Bethesda, Maryland, who was surveyed at the Women's March in 2018, listed "our corrupt President," "the environment," and "civil rights and the rule of law" as the top three issues facing our country. All three of her responses focused on how electoral politics would solve the problem. Her solution to the civil rights issue was to "elect people who understand the rule of law and respect [the] civil rights of all people." Alisa, a forty-one-year-old white woman from Shippensburg, Pennsylvania, originally surveyed at the March For Our Lives in March 2018, also listed civil rights as one of the top issues facing America. To solve this problem Alisa wrote: "We need to find all of the racist law enforcement officers and politicians and remove them from positions of power. [And] we need to better educate people on race issues." In Alisa's solution, electoral politics was intertwined with more options that address civil rights in America.

AFTER THE ELECTION

Responses to this question in the November survey, two days *after* the midterm elections, were less focused on electoral politics. Individuals wrote in 472 individual responses (just like the May survey, everyone did not provide three solutions). Many solutions noted the need for a different administration, and a number of solutions in the postelection survey focused on impeaching President Trump, which was similar to the results of the May survey. Many of the numerous suggestions that referenced the need to remove the Trump administration from office specifically mentioned the Mueller investigation into Russia's potential interference in the 2016 election and possible collusion with the Trump campaign. Taken together, these solutions represented 9 percent of all options offered by survey respondents in November 2018.

Other Resisters continued to focus on electoral change, looking toward the 2020 elections to address the most pressing issues. Sixteen solutions specifically mentioned the 2020 elections or electoral politics as the means for solving the top issues facing the United States, and eight mentioned the need for Democrats to hold the majority in both houses of the U.S. Congress and the presidency. These electoral solutions represented 5 percent of all the suggestions on how to solve the top issues facing the United States.

The most frequent solutions offered after the midterm elections, however, specifically referenced more progressive types of social change. Four people wrote in "socialism" as a solution to the top issues facing America, and thirty-three additional solutions were offered that explicitly listed aspects of social democratic policy, such as nationalizing industries, redistributing wealth, and limiting capitalism. Almost all of the solutions to the health care issue (the number three issue) focused on a more socialized form of medical coverage that guaranteed health care for all citizens. The overwhelming majority of responses by Resisters concerned about health care mentioned "single-payer health care" or "Medicare for all." These more progressive solutions represented 21 percent of all options offered.

The changing focus on the *types* of solutions suggested is apparent when we look at how individual respondent's solutions changed between May and November. Thirty-eight percent of respondents who participated in both waves of the follow-up survey shifted their focus from institutional political options to more progressive alternatives consistent with social democratic policies. This shift in focus from mainstream political strategies connected to elections and the legislative system to more progressive strategies was a consistent trend across Resisters who had been surveyed at every march.[30]

This level of mainstream support for more socially democratic policies is in contrast to the limited support for such solutions offered by Resisters six months before the midterm elections. The shift is particularly notable because many people changed their perspective over the six-month period. In fact, not one person had written in "socialism" or "social democracy" as a solution to the top issues facing the United States in May 2018. A small number of responders mentioned aspects of social democratic policies, including options such as "redistributive policies" and "Medicare for all." In addition, nine people had written "eliminate capitalism" as a solution in May. Together these solutions represented about 7 percent of all solutions offered six months before the midterm elections versus representing 21 percent of all solutions after the midterm elections.

The shift in perspective can be seen in the case of Brian, a thirty-one-year-old white man from Washington, D.C. originally surveyed at the March for Science who wrote: "Flip the House of Representatives to Democratic control" as the solution to all three of his top issues: Trump, civil rights, and women's rights. After the midterm elections he added "income inequality" to his list of top issues and listed the solution as a "minimum wage that is an actual living wage."

Paul, a forty-year-old from Williamsburg, Virginia,[31] initially surveyed at the People's Climate March, named inequality as a top issue facing America six months before the midterms. Before the election he wrote that "progressive policies" were the best solution to the issue. After the election, he continued to consider inequality as one of the top issues, but his solution was much more specific and involved a suite of socially democratic initiatives: "Reverse tax breaks for the wealthy, invest in free/ affordable education for all (including pre-K and higher education), and Medicaid for all." Similarly, Sandy, a fifty-six-year-old multiracial woman who traveled from San Antonio, Texas, to attend the March For Our Lives, wrote "Change Congress/ the President" as the solution for all three of her top issues facing America in May. After the election, however, she offered two more specific solutions: "provide insurance to everyone" and "raise the minimum wage."

In many cases, solutions addressed numerous issues simultaneously. For example, Janet, a thirty-two-year-old white woman from Arlington, Virginia, originally surveyed at the March for Science in April 2017, embedded the issue of civil rights into her solution for problems with the American political system. Her solutions in May focused on change through legislation, but these solutions changed after the election: "Get rid of the GOP, Nazis, racists. Or limit their power by addressing voting rights, gerrymandering, etc." Similarly, the solutions offered by Katherine, a sixty-five-year-old from Philadelphia originally surveyed at the 2017 Women's March, became more progressive after the election. In May she said we need to "get money out of politics" to fix the political system. After the midterm elections, however, her solutions were more specific about the steps needed to solve the problems she saw with the political system in America: "Undo the recent tax cut, reform our economic structure, strengthen public schools across the country, reduce the cost of attending community college, dramatically increase public funding for technical education in clean energy industry." Although Katherine was specifically addressing problems she identified with the political system, her solutions integrated what she saw as issues with the economy, our education system, and the environment.

Janelle, a twenty-eight-year-old black woman surveyed at the March for Racial Justice who said she worked for a nongovernmental organization in the Washington, D.C. area, specifically listed the environment as a top issue facing the United States. After the midterms, her solutions to environmental issues also addressed challenges she saw with the economic system: "We need a major shift in our economic system and mode of production to even have a chance to save ourselves from the impending environmental catastrophe caused by the capitalist mode of production."

A number of environmental solutions referenced the notion of a "Green New Deal" program, which surged in popularity after the election. Before the election, Seth, a forty-one-year-old white man who traveled from New York City to attend the People's Climate March in 2017, said that global agreements and conservation should be used to solve environmental problems. After the election, his perspective shifted, and he proposed "massive federal and state spending. But that is also an economic stimulus." John, a thirty-four-year-old white man from Washington, D.C. also originally surveyed at the People's Climate March, provided additional details: "To create a green jobs program investing in building renewable energy capacity, storage, and needed infrastructure around the country. Include with this a range of synchronized policies that move to electrify transportation, make transportation without cars feasible in communities, and make the system conduct the choices instead of creating guilt for individual citizens in 'not doing their part.'"

A number of solutions offered after the midterms to solve environmental issues were similar to the responses in May and focused on institutional politics. For example, nine solutions stated that instituting a carbon tax would solve environmental problems like climate change. Eight solutions mentioned the need for the United States to reengage in the international Paris Agreement, which President Trump withdrew from in the summer of 2017 amid criticism at home and abroad.

Participants in the Families Belong Together event did not participate in the first wave of the follow-up survey because the event had not yet taken place. These Resisters were surveyed in November and offered solutions to the top issues facing America that followed a similar pattern. They included a number of references to options that focused on implementing more socialist policies, such as raising the minimum wage, increasing taxes, and implementing universal health care. Overall, across participants from all of the events over the first two years of the Trump administration, there was a clear shift to more progressive social democratic solutions after the midterm elections.

MOVING FORWARD

The evidence presented in this chapter illustrates how the resistance in the streets redirected its attention to the districts in the lead-up to the 2018 midterm elections. Resisters worked to affect social change via the midterm elections: they signed petitions, they donated money, they went to town hall meetings, they canvassed, they phone banked, they wrote postcards, and they gave countless hours to resistance groups, the Democratic Party, and individual campaigns to help make the blue wave a reality. Although their work varied from group to group, the degree to which they engaged in resistance in the districts is a testament to their focus. It also provides evidence of the effectiveness of the distributed organizing strategies employed by resistance groups to channel interest, enthusiasm, and outrage into the work needed in communities and districts for the midterm elections.

In the wake of the 2018 election, Resisters continue to see numerous problems facing the United States. With a sense that social change is still needed, many participants in the Resistance are now looking beyond institutional politics to make their visions of social change a reality. The shift in perspective from institutional solutions that focus on electoral politics to structural solutions that focus on the way the American economy is structured makes a lot of sense given how long political change can take. These changes include implementing a number of social democratic policies to address the top issues facing the United States.

The Trump administration has worked nonstop since taking office to shrink the U.S. government and to curtail its social and environmental programs. It is not a surprise that Resisters would look to social change from outside the political system that has empowered the president. This shift in focus is reminiscent of previous periods in U.S. history when the public has pushed for more socialist policies, with limited success.[32]

Given the priorities of the members of the Resistance, newly elected political officials and organizations looking for support would be wise to think about how to integrate these concerns into their work. With environmental issues, including climate change, dominating the list, candidates and groups looking for people willing to put in the time in the streets and in the districts should think about appealing directly to these concerns. Moreover, anyone hoping to harness the energy of the Resistance should seriously consider what the shift in focus from mainstream institutional political solutions to more progressive social democratic ones means to progressive politics in the United States and to the movement itself.

Chapter Five

LOOKING BACK WHILE
MARCHING FORWARD

I MET LINDA SARSOUR (a co-chair of the National Women's March) at the CNN studios in Washington, D.C. early in the morning of the third Women's March in January 2019. Linda was there to talk about the group's new policy agenda and the 2019 demonstration, which was scheduled to start later that morning. I had been invited to provide insights about the individuals who were participating and to put them in the context of the American Resistance. After my brief segment and a chat with Linda and the other guests about what they expected during the day's events, I put on my coat, picked up my bag of pink data collection tablets, and went out into the cold morning to survey protesters once again.

I met my research team of undergraduates and graduate students—all women—at a coffee shop near Metro Center, and we walked into the streets to study the crowds. Unlike the first two Women's Marches, the reason to participate in the third event was less clear. There wasn't a new person in the White House, there wasn't a national election coming up in the fall, and Sarsour and the other leaders of the National Women's March group were under fire for "allegations of anti-Semitism, secretive financial dealings, infighting, and disputes over who gets to own and define the Women's March."[1] Moreover, the weather was expected to get nasty with sleet and ice predicted in Washington, D.C., and worse all over the Northeast. With so many headwinds, I anticipated a less impressive turnout than the previous two years.

Since I was coming from my 7 a.m. interview on CNN, I was wearing TV makeup and fake eyelashes for the first time in my life, it was definitely the most put together I have ever looked when surveying a crowd at a demonstration. This level of glamor in the streets was not without challenges as I found it hard not to blink repeatedly when I was talking to potential research subjects and, if I touched my face, my glove would turn orange from the layers of makeup they had applied.

In contrast to my meager expectations, the third Women's March turned out an estimated one hundred thousand people in Washington, D.C., which was 25 percent larger than the second Women's March in 2018.[2] Like the previous marches in the Resistance chronicled in this book, this march turned out more women than men, and protesters came from a highly educated portion of the U.S. population. Participants at the third Women's March were motivated by a range of issues, and all motivations were very high: 80 percent of participants listed women's rights as a reason for joining the event, and 76 percent of the crowd said they were motivated by President Trump and his policies. This heightened focus on President Trump may have been because the Women's March in 2019 took place on the twenty-eighth day of the longest federal shutdown in U.S. history (the second Women's March took place on the first day of a two-day government shutdown). Only two of the fourteen motivations that emerged from all the participants at the 2017 Women's March—labor and religion—were not identified by at least half of the crowd at the 2019 Women's March as motivations for attending the event.

Consistent with other large events in the American Resistance, attendees at the 2019 Women's March reported doing much more than marching in the streets; they also were active in politics in their communities. Three-quarters of the participants followed the advice of numerous resistance groups (and many others) and voted in the midterm elections. This rate of voting is substantially higher than the 49 percent turnout in the 2018 election, which experts had reported broke records.[3] Many of the participants in the third Women's March did even more than vote: 44 percent also reported working with the Democratic Party before the 2018 midterm elections, and 28 percent reported working with an individual candidate's campaign. They donated money, canvassed, wrote postcards, and phone banked for candidates in their communities and in congressional districts around the country. Donald Trump is facing his second two years in office with a House of Representatives led by his opposition due, in part, to these efforts.

WHAT COMES AFTER THE BLUE WAVE?

The success of the Democrats in the midterm elections made me wonder whether the Resistance would become the next movement to join the graveyard of Democratic politics.[4] History suggests that progressive political movements lose their potency after Democratic electoral wins. One has only to look at the post-9/11 antiwar movement and the Obama campaign in 2008 for evidence.[5] Although some called the campaign to elect Barack Obama a movement to elect the first black president, the campaign's infrastructure—which became Organizing for America after President Obama took office and has since shifted to become Organizing for Action[6]—was quickly subsumed into the Democratic Party after the inauguration. In *Groundbreakers*, Elizabeth McKenna, Hahrie Han, and Jeremy Bird provide an in-depth study of the ground game of Barack Obama's two presidential campaigns, noting how the campaign's organizational culture changed from 2008 to the 2012 reelection campaign. They note that respondents reported "the focus on the numbers of door knocks, voter registration forms, and phone calls overshadowed the relational dimension of organizing that had set OFA [Obama for America] apart."[7] This account provides more evidence that the army of activists celebrated in 2008 as the future of grassroots organizing had been asked to refocus on metrics, becoming an army of bean counters. With Democrats enjoying a majority in the House of Representatives, there is a precedent for the flame of the American Resistance to fizzle out entirely or to meet a similar fate.

Throughout the first two years of the Trump administration, Americans took to the streets by the millions to
express their opposition to Trump and his policies.[8] Their
persistence is due, in part, to the degree to which President
Trump himself has fanned the flames of Resistance with his
policies and his public attacks on institutions (both inside
and outside the U.S. government), as well as his attacks on
individuals on social media. The Resistance is a product of
the president's behavior combined with the response by
Americans to an out-of-touch Democratic Party and the
reach of conservative dark money in politics. The American
Resistance emerged in the aftermath of the 2016 election,
and it has flourished.

After participating in many large-scale protests, the outrage
and enthusiasm of the Resistance was channeled back into communities and congressional districts leading up to the midterm
elections. Recall that six months before the midterm elections
participants in the resistance in the streets identified electoral
politics generally, and the midterm elections specifically, as the
main solution to what they considered to be the "top challenges"
facing the United States. During the 2018 election cycle, individuals got involved with resistance groups in manifold ways.
In addition, they worked with individual candidate's campaigns
and through the Democratic Party with a good deal of focus
on local political groups and efforts. The fact that most resisters
who reported being involved with the Democratic Party also
reported helping out with at least one individual candidate's
campaign before the 2018 election is remarkable. These findings
provide more evidence to support the claims of Lara Putnam

and Theda Skocpol that Democrats are rebuilding the party from the local level up.[9]

The result of these efforts was a midterm election that saw unprecedented turnout and enthusiasm, particularly by educated white women who make up the bulk of the Resistance.[10] The electoral success of the Resistance provides an example of how movements can be redirected from "the barricades to the ballots" in this era of distributed organizing.[11] The large protests served to create a sense of collective identity.[12] Rather than being the end result of social movement activity, however; these protests were part of the mobilization process to take action in communities and congressional districts in a countermovement against the Trump administration and its policies.

The American Resistance is in stark contrast to the earlier observations by Doug McAdam and Karina Kloos in *Deeply Divided* that "the vast majority of social movements exert little or no effect on parties. In truth, most movements have no interest in engaging with parties or national politics more generally."[13] Although the role the Resistance is playing in the Democratic Party is unclear, between work with resistance groups and individual campaigns, there is no question that the Resistance contributed substantially to national politics around the 2018 election.

Since its beginning in 2017, the American Resistance has combined unconventional forms of contentious politics with more institutional forms of electoral politics to challenge the Trump administration and its policies, and it has met with a good deal of success.[14] But what happens to a movement that has been laser-focused on a single election when that election is over? Can a movement that has aimed so much attention on electoral goals successfully shift to less institutional politics? Or will the American Resistance follow the trajectory of the post-9/11 antiwar movement? Heaney and Rojas detailed the results of that movement: "grassroots mobilizations diminished considerably after substantial Democratic gains in the 2006 congressional midterm elections," and the antiwar movement collapsed "after the election of President Barack Obama" in 2008.[15]

The success of the Resistance has been facilitated by groups employing distributed organizing to get the job done in innovative ways, engaging individuals and organizations to work for social change in the streets, in their communities, and in congressional districts around the country. Distributed organizing has contributed to a transformation of what organizational membership means in the United States, making it more difficult to trace the influence of organizations in this movement. Distributed organizing did not initiate these changes in membership, but as groups increasingly shift their strategies to focus on a more fluid type of membership, the implications of these changes are notable.[16] This style of membership increases the reach of these groups by lowering the barriers to entry, but this change has real consequences for the degree to which individuals develop a sense of collective identity or brand loyalty to the organizations that claim them as members.

Resistance Groups have implemented various forms of distributed organizing that capitalize on digital tools to facilitate fluid membership into loosely coordinated networks of interested individuals who are geographically dispersed. Harnessing the capacity of distributed organizing has empowered these groups to maintain a local focus even as it leverages the efforts of people who are not local (but might be near local). Resisters have volunteered their time in person and from afar through technological innovations that make it possible to phone bank or text bank from anywhere to everywhere in the United States, whenever it is needed most.

Utilizing a less federated structure that capitalizes on the energy and enthusiasm of individuals, channeling it to where it is needed most, makes a lot of sense. However, the geographically dispersed activism facilitated by distributed organizing has the potential to continue broader trends in American civic life, which are changing the structure of groups and the degree to which groups build interpersonal connections that lead to political infrastructure in communities that endure. As I discussed in *Activism, Inc.*, the Left had been moving away from face-to-face relational politics for years.[17] The Obama campaigns provided a countertrend, but distributed organizing has empowered groups to continue this broader trend away from local connections. In *Digitally Enabled Social Change*, Jennifer Earl and Katrina Kimport focus specifically on how internet-based technologies have been changing the dynamics of organizing and protest. Technological innovation has lowered the cost of protest and facilitated engaging in collective action despite the absence of geographic proximity.[18] Based on my observations of the American Resistance, distributed organizing is amplifying these trends.

Organizing the more than sixty groups that worked together on The Last Weekend was made possible by the digital tools of distributed organizing. The effort was successful in part because individuals were contacted via the membership lists of these sixty groups to mobilize people and channel them directly into efforts around the election, but there may be some unintended side effects. Rather than the local face-to-face work that has been found to win campaigns and make lasting social connections, distributed organizing is making it all too easy to corral interested individuals into telemarketing jobs for our country's future.[19]

FROM THE 116TH CONGRESS TO THE 2020 ELECTIONS

During my interviews in October 2018, many leaders of resistance groups told me that they planned to continue to channel their members' outrage against the president and his administration after the election. Even with their strong intentions, however, it was unclear whether the ground troops would follow their lead. In the days after the election, I worried that the Resistance would be another political loss, but I didn't have to worry for long.

I was not surprised (but strangely heartened) to find that the outrage continued after the midterms. Moral outrage played a large role in motivating many Americans to become involved in the Resistance, including individuals without strong ties to the groups that were organizing events. These findings were corroborated in a study of the 2017 Women's March by Rachel McKane and Holly McCammon, who concluded that protest participants at the hundreds of sister marches "often did not need movement organizational leaders to raise consciousness and help them define their grievances and sense of threat."[20] This outrage is amplified by what Jeffrey Berry and Sarah Sobieraj documented in *Outrage Industry*, which found that the political media is increasingly fueling scandal; it has sustained the activism of the Resistance throughout the president's first twenty-four months in office, even after organizers themselves were reporting that people are sick of marching on Washington.[21]

As President Trump continues to mobilize his base with inflammatory rhetoric and extremist politics, he may be exactly what the Resistance needs to survive. For example, on the day after the midterm elections, the president fired Attorney General Jeff Sessions and installed someone who did not support the Mueller investigation. Almost immediately, MoveOn coordinated #ProtectMueller actions with the help of a number of other resistance groups, including Indivisible, the National Women's March group, and March On, to take to the streets and show their disapproval of the president's actions. With just twenty-four hours' notice, the event turned out tens of thousands of people at more than eight hundred locations around the United States.[22] Less than a month later, in honor of the 116th Congress taking office and despite the partial government shutdown, Indivisible hosted a day of action on January 3, 2019, that turned out members from its local groups to participate in 168 events in thirty-one states. Leah Greenberg, co-executive director of Indivisible, told me that this day was "Indivisible's largest legislative day of action so far."[23]

The 2019 Women's March in more than three hundred cities and towns, a Youth Week of Action focused on town halls protesting gun violence that commemorated the anniversary of the 2018 Walkout for Gun Violence, and a youth climate strike in more than one hundred cities around the United States[24] provide ample evidence that the outrage that mobilized loosely affiliated (as well as completely unaffiliated) individuals to get out in the streets, march in opposition, and more is not going away any time soon. People continue to march in the streets, do die-ins in their town squares, confront their elected officials at town hall meetings, and hold their elected officials accountable. It is a bitter irony that both the president's base and the American Resistance feed off of Trump's outrageous conduct.

The Resistance has persisted beyond the midterm elections, but so too have the internal divisions in the Democratic Party. In fact, one week after the midterm elections, the congressional Black Caucus passed a vote of no confidence in DNC chairman Tom Perez over differing opinions about the roles of local party representatives, party officials, and members of Congress.[25] A few weeks after that, more divisions were made public as the national party fought with its state affiliates over the party's voter data file, which is a key tool for electoral campaigns and other Left-leaning political groups.[26] More recently, tensions within the Democratic Party attracted media attention when Representative Alexandra Ocasio-Cortez, who won her seat as a primary challenger to a Democratic incumbent, announced that she would support primary challengers to more moderate Democratic incumbents.[27]

Cracks in the coalition that has supported the Resistance since the 2017 Women's March have become more apparent as well. In the lead-up to the Women's March in 2019, tensions among the coalition of groups that had supported previous Women's Marches gained attention when some groups decided not to endorse the march and some cities decided not to hold marches to commemorate the third anniversary. Media airtime focused on a number of issues, including claims of anti-Semitism by the leadership of the National Women's March group, as well as who owns the name the "Women's March" itself,[28] rather than the hundreds of thousands of people who headed back into the streets once again.

MARCHING TOWARD 2020

The challenges facing the Democratic Party and the tensions within the groups that make up the Resistance raise questions about the degree to which a countermovement fueled by distributed organizing can replace the federated structure of the bygone days of civic America. Can technological innovation overcome the erosion of local infrastructure and save people from bowling alone and campaigning with only astroturf in much of the country? Moreover, it is unclear how distributed organizing will be able to combine geographically scattered activism with face-to-face connections among community members in meaningful ways that survive the latest elections and political campaigns.[29]

In 2020, distributed organizing on the Left will go head to head with the Trump campaign and the Republican Party in an effort to take back the Senate and win the presidency from Donald Trump. Some are already predicting that the Democrats are likely to be losers in that contest. As Democratic digital strategist Tara McGowan noted in February 2019: "Trump is already winning."[30] In March 2019, the *Washington Post* described the ways that the Trump campaign will capitalize on its digital volunteer infrastructure: "[It] plans to enlist more than 1 million volunteers using [a] vast database of supporters who have attended Trump's raucous political rallies over the past two years."[31] Although it is possible to envision the fragile coalition on the Left holding through 2020, it is unclear how effective they will be in working together against the GOP machine.

The Democratic field for 2020 is populated by candidates representing a range of ideological approaches and backgrounds. Positions of most candidates have definitely moved to the Left of the 2016 platform and seem to reflect priorities expressed by the American Resistance. If the Democratic Party selects a more centrist candidate as their nominee once again, the American Resistance could be marginalized in the 2020 election.[32]

So far, though, the shift to the Left has been resonating throughout the Democratic Party and can be seen in the work of the Democratic-led House of Representatives in the 116th Congress. The Green New Deal has attracted a lot of attention, along with intense scrutiny, since it was officially introduced by Representative Ocasio-Cortez and Senator Markey in February 2019. Beyond these more provocative efforts, the House of Representatives has passed the "For the People Act of 2019," which aims to address dark money and "get money out of politics."[33] These initiatives are particularly interesting because they focus on the top two issues Resisters listed as facing Americans in the survey after the midterm elections: the environment and the political system.

Neither of these congressional efforts has a chance of passing through the Republican dominated Senate or being signed by President Trump, but these issues are being discussed by most of the Democratic presidential hopefuls who have announced their campaigns for the 2020 election. By March 2019, *Roll Call* reported that "every Democratic White House contender has taken a no-corporate-PAC pledge." In other words, as James Hohmann writes in the *Washington Post*, "Bernie Sanders sounds less 'radical' than he did in 2016 because Democrats have moved his way."[34]

It is impossible to predict how the Democratic field will play out in the 2020 election. The American Resistance has channeled the energy and enthusiasm of a large group of progressive Americans to participate in our democracy in specific and effective ways, so whoever wins the nomination would do well to capitalize on their efforts. Collaboration among a presidential campaign, the Democratic Party, and resistance groups could extend the distributed organizing model to cultivate a strong progressive infrastructure in American communities. If successful, it will leave as its legacy a lasting root structure when the 2020 election is behind us.

Taking the survey at the 2019 Women's March.

Photograph courtesy of Emily Rasinski for the University of Maryland.

METHODOLOGICAL
APPENDIX

THIS PROJECT utilized a multi-staged, mixed-methods approach
to understanding the American Resistance. The data were
obtained through two types of surveys (direct in-person data
collection in the streets at protest events and two Internet-based
follow-up surveys) as well as through open-ended, semistructured interviews with representatives of resistance groups.
Survey data were initially collected in the streets at all of the
large-scale (twenty-five thousand people or more) protest
events in Washington, D.C. during the first two years of the
Trump administration (from the Women's March the day after
the inauguration in January 2017 to the midterm elections in
November 2018). Data were collected by surveying protest participants during the events and was augmented by two rounds
of follow-up surveys administered to individuals who expressed
a willingness to participate in follow-up research. In addition,
open-ended, semistructured interviews were conducted with

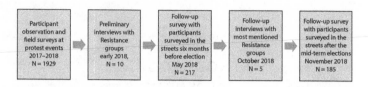

FIGURE A.1 Data Collection Flowchart
Source: Author's own data.

leaders of resistance groups at the beginning of 2018. Follow-up interviews were conducted in October with representatives from those groups that were most frequently named in the follow-up survey and by other groups in May 2018. Figure A.1 presents a flowchart of data collected for this project. In the sections that follow, each source is discussed separately.

SURVEYING THE RESISTANCE IN THE STREETS

INITIAL SURVEY AT LARGE-SCALE PROTEST EVENTS

Participants at all seven events described in chapter 2 were randomly sampled and surveyed. Snaking through the crowd as people assembled, researchers "counted off" protesters while participants were lining up and listening to speeches. Members of the research team selected every fifth person to participate as determined by researchers working in a particular section. Members of the research team were placed in the crowd at incremental positions to gather data throughout the space. This method avoids the potential of selection bias by preventing researchers from selecting only "approachable peers."[1]

The sampling methodology was consistent with other studies of street demonstrations in the United States and abroad that use a field approximation of random selection at protest events.[2] Given the large size of the crowds and the labor-intensive nature of the survey methodology, the samples represent small, randomized portions of the overall participant populations at each demonstration.

In all cases, data were collected with a research team so that sampling could take place throughout the staging areas for each event. Each march was unique, and the research team size varied at each event. The sampling methodology was tailored to suit each protest.

Women's March 2017. In January 2017, an eight-member research team entered the crowd at the entrances designated by the organizers and sampled march participants throughout the morning and early afternoon while the rally took place. Researchers completed 530 surveys with a refusal rate of 8 percent. Data were collected on a one-page, two-sided paper survey that respondents filled out in the field.

March for Science. In April 2017, a twelve-member research team entered the staging area around the Washington Monument. March participants were sampled throughout the morning and early afternoon as they listened to speeches about the importance of science. To expedite data collection and analysis, data were collected on tablet computers rather than paper surveys at this all subsequent marches. The research team was pulled early because the tablets we had just begun using for data collection were malfunctioning in the rain, and I didn't want to risk losing data already collected. Even with these challenges, researchers completed 212 surveys with a refusal rate of 6 percent. However, the data yielded only 201 usable surveys due to data loss from malfunctioning tablets.

People's Climate March. In April 2017, a ten-member research team entered the crowd in the designated areas around the National Mall. March participants were sampled throughout the morning and early afternoon as they lined up to march. Researchers completed 351 surveys with a refusal rate of 11 percent.

March for Racial Justice. In September 2017, a fourteen-member research team entered the crowd in the designated areas around Lincoln Park. Participants were sampled throughout the morning and early afternoon during the rally. Researchers completed 185 surveys with a refusal rate of 17 percent.

Women's March 2018. In January 2018, a six-member research team entered the crowd at the various entrances to the reflecting pool and steps of the Lincoln Memorial and sampled march participants throughout the morning and early afternoon while the rally took place. Researchers completed 205 surveys with a refusal rate of 8 percent.

March For Our Lives. In March 2018, a six-member research team entered the crowd at the various entrances on Pennsylvania Avenue and sampled participants throughout the morning and early afternoon while the rally/concert took place. Researchers completed 256 surveys with a refusal rate of 7 percent.

Families Belong Together. In June 2018, a four-member research team entered the crowd at the various entrances to Lafayette Square right next to the White House and sampled rally participants throughout the morning and early afternoon while the rally took place. Researchers completed 201 surveys with a refusal rate of 9 percent.

These refusal rates are consistent with other studies that use this methodology and are substantially lower than studies that rely on mailed in questionnaires, which can suffer from delayed refusal bias.[3]

The survey was designed to be short and noninvasive to encourage the highest level of participation possible and to facilitate data collection in the field. Participants were able to complete the survey in about ten minutes.[4] An additional question was added after each march to measure the number of participants that had attended the previous large-scale events in the Resistance. All survey data were collected in accordance with the University of Maryland policies instituted by their Institutional Review Board (UMD IRB Protocol # 999342–1). Only individuals over the age of eighteen were eligible to participate in the study.

FOLLOW-UP SURVEYS WITH SAMPLE OF RESISTERS IN THE STREETS

Two waves of the follow-up survey were administered: the first in May, six months before the 2018 midterm elections; the second in November, two days after the midterm elections. Follow-up surveys were distributed to anyone who had indicated on the initial survey that he or she was willing to participate and provided an email address.[5] The first follow-up survey included protesters from the 2017 Women's March through the 2018 March For Our Lives. The second follow-up survey included protesters from the 2017 Women's March through the 2018 Families Belong Together event (see table A.1).

For the May 2018 follow-up survey, 841 people surveyed in the streets provided email contacts and agreed to participate in the first follow-up survey, but only 777 of those email addresses worked in May. In addition, 21 respondents chose to opt out of the survey when they received it. The 756 people who provided working email addresses and were willing to participate represented 44 percent of the people who had participated in surveys

TABLE A.1 Follow-up response rates by march where initially surveyed (in percent)

	Participated in follow-up survey May 2018*	Participated in follow-up survey November 2018*
Women's March 2017	18	18
March for Science	29	23
People's Climate March	25	19
March for Racial Justice	32	27
Women's March 2018	44	29
March For Our Lives	40	20
Families Belong Together	—	29

*Numbers in percent; rates are calculated based on the percentage of those who expressed a willingness to participate, shared their contact information, and did not opt out of the study.

Source: Author's own data.

while they were marching in the streets. For the November 2018 follow-up survey, 938 people surveyed in the streets provided email contacts, but only 865 of those email addresses worked in November. In addition, 40 respondents chose to opt out of the survey when they received it. The 825 people who provided working email addresses and were willing to participate represented 43 percent of the people who had participated in surveys while they were marching in the streets.

All data for the follow-up surveys were collected in accordance with University of Maryland-Collect Park Institutional Review Board Protocol #999342-2. Data were collected through the online survey system *Qualtrics*. Each follow-up survey was fielded for three weeks (beginning May 7 and November 8). During that time, multiple prompts and reminders were sent. In total, 217 people participated in the first follow-up survey, representing a 29 percent response rate, and 185 participated in the second follow-up survey, representing a 22 percent response rate. The difference in response rates between May and November was likely due to two factors: the increasing time difference between when protesters were originally surveyed and the follow-up surveys and the activities of resistance groups who were bombarding Resisters with post-midterm election follow-up emails requesting input on their postelection plans and asking for a donation.[6]

Response rates varied based on when the respondent was initially surveyed, with participants in earlier marches yielding a lower response rate than those at more recent events. Response rates for the May follow-up ranged from a low of 18 percent for participants from the 2017 Women's March to a high of 44 percent for participants for the 2018 Women's March. These rates are consistent with my previous work employing follow-up surveys with protesters: response rates decline with the increasing gap between initial contact and the follow-up request.[7] The November survey suffered from the growing gap between when people were initially surveyed and when they were asked to participate in the follow-up survey. It had been twenty-three months since the people at the 2017 Women's March had answered my questions at the march itself. Response rates for the November 2018 follow-up survey ranged from a low of 18 percent at the 2017 Women's March to a high of 29 percent for participants at the Families Belong Together event in June 2018.

Even with these differences in response rate, the samples from the two follow-up surveys are similar to the full sample of participants in the resistance in the streets: there are no statistically significant differences in gender, age, or race.[8] Data collected in the streets and in the follow-up samples are more female and more white than the general population. However, the participants in the May and November follow-ups are more educated than the overall sample and are less likely to be first-time protesters. In addition, participants in the November follow-up were more Left-leaning than the original sample of protesters.

The follow-up surveys included questions about which protests respondents had attended, their levels of civic engagement, and what groups they had worked with since the Women's March in 2017. Additional questions were added to the November follow-up survey asking how respondents had worked with the Democratic Party and with individual candidate's campaigns before the election. Both follow-up surveys included open-ended questions about the top three issues facing the United States and what respondents believed were the best ways to solve the problems they named. I hand coded these open-ended responses into the categories discussed in chapter 4. Pseudonyms are used when quoting any open-ended responses from surveys to protect the privacy of Resisters who shared their opinions.

INTERVIEW DATA

In addition to the extensive data on protesters, I interviewed the leaders of national resistance groups in the winter of 2018. Groups were initially identified through media mentions and by other resistance groups involved in organizing the resistance in the streets. Groups that were most frequently named in the first follow-up survey in May 2018 were approached in October to participate in a follow-up interview a month before the midterm elections. In addition, one group was added because other groups mentioned the group many times during follow-up interviews. All interview data were collected in accordance with the University of Maryland's policies on research on human subjects (UMD IRB Protocol #878998-2).

Initial interviews included questions regarding the personal background of the group leaders and the history of each group. Interviews lasted from forty-five minutes to one and a half hours in length. I asked representatives of these resistance groups to discuss the work the group was doing to mobilize grassroots participants to work on campaigns in their communities and/or around the election. When applicable, I also asked representatives how their work was different from what the group had done during the 2016 election cycle. In addition, I asked who the groups' main collaborators and opponents were.

During the follow-up interviews in October, I asked group representatives how their work and their approaches to engaging with the grass roots had changed as the election drew closer. I included questions about the scale of the work the group was focused on in the lead-up to the midterm elections to gauge whether the groups were working at the local, state, and/or federal level. Finally, I asked representatives to discuss their group's approach to distributed organizing.

These interviews were open-ended and semistructured. The purpose of the semistructured interviewing technique, as summarized by John Lofland and Lyn Lofland, is "to achieve analyses that (1) are attuned to aspects of human group life, (2) depict aspects of that life, and (3) provide perspectives on that life that are simply not available to or prompted by other methods of research."[9] The interviews were recorded and transcribed, and extensive notes and memos from all of the interviews were kept as the bulk of the qualitative data set. A qualitative data analysis computer program (QSR NVivo11) was used to store, sort, and code transcribed data. As the patterns across cases emerged, I distinguished between first-order conclusions (i.e., those explicitly drawn or stated by the respondent) and second-order conclusions (i.e., those drawn from what was said). In so doing, I acknowledge my role in interpreting the data patterns as well as subjecting the respondents' claims to additional scrutiny.

Quotations from the interviews have been edited to remove repetitive phrases and words (e.g., y'know, like, um, and kind of) that had no bearing on the content of the statements. Quotations from those who declined direct attribution are referenced without naming the individual or his or her group.

NOTES

1. HOW DID WE GET HERE?

1. Greg Waldman and Greg Sargent, "Obama Just Delivered His Answer to Trump's Authoritarianism," *Washington Post*, September 7, 2018. The full transcript is available at https://www.usatoday.com/story/news/politics /elections/2018/09/07/president-barack-obamas-speech-transcript -slamming-trump/1225554002/.
2. Victoria Kaplan, interview with author, October 12, 2018.
3. The Last Weekend coalition, https://thelastweekend.org/, accessed October 30, 2018.
4. These observations are consistent with the limited work on the Resistance thus far. See Lara Putnam and Theda Skocpol, "Middle America Reboots Democracy," *Democracy Journal*, February 20, 2018, https:// democracyjournal.org/arguments/middle-america-reboots-democracy/; David S. Meyer and Sidney Tarrow, *The Resistance: The Dawn of the Anti-Trump Opposition Movement* (New York: Oxford University Press, 2018).
5. Voting results are available at https://www.elections.virginia.gov/results reports/registration-statistics/registrationturnout-statistics/index.html, accessed January 2, 2018. See also Jenna Portnoy, "Democrat Jennifer T. Wexton Defeats Rep. Barbara Comstock, Turning a GOP Stronghold District in Virginia Blue," *Washington Post*, November 6, 2018.

6. Campaign coordinator email correspondence with author, 2018.

7. Anonymous, "Opinion | I Am Part of the Resistance Inside the Trump Administration," *New York Times*, September 5, 2018, https://www.nytimes.com/interactive/2017/admin/100000006089332.embedded.html/.

8. For a discussion, see Sidney Tarrow, "Rhythms of Resistance: The Anti-Trumpian Movement in a Cycle of Contention," in *The Resistance: The Dawn of the Anti-Trump Opposition Movement*, ed. David S. Meyer and Sidney Tarrow (New York: Oxford University Press, 2018), 187–206; Sidney Tarrow and David S. Meyer, "The Challenges of the Anti-Trump Movement," *Partecipazione e Conflitto* 11, no. 3 (2018): 614–45.

9. For an overview of countermovements, see David S. Meyer and Suzanne Staggenborg, "Movements, Countermovements, and the Structure of Political Opportunity," *American Journal of Sociology* 101, no. 6 (1996): 1628–60; Tahi L. Mottl, "The Analysis of Countermovements," *Social Problems* 27, no. 5 (1980): 620–35.

10. For a discussion of challenges stemming from the merging of movements, see Dana R. Fisher, "COP-15 in Copenhagen: How the Merging of Movements Left Civil Society Out in the Cold," *Global Environmental Politics* 10, no. 2 (2010): 11–17. For an overview of coalitions and their challenges, see Margaret Levi and Gillian H. Murphy, "Coalitions of Contention: The Case of the WTO Protests in Seattle," *Political Studies* 54, no. 4 (December 1, 2006): 651–70, https://doi.org/10.1111/j.1467-9248.2006.00629.x; Nella Van Dyke and Holly J. McCammon, *Strategic Alliances: Coalition Building and Social Movements* (Minneapolis: University of Minnesota Press, 2010).

11. Farah Stockman, "One Year After Women's March, More Activism but Less Unity," *New York Times*, January 15, 2018, https://www.nytimes.com/2018/01/15/us/womens-march-anniversary.html; Farah Stockman, "Women's March Roiled by Accusations of Anti-Semitism," *New York Times*, December 24, 2018, https://www.nytimes.com/2018/12/23/us/womens-march-anti-semitism.html.

12. These examples are not meant to be exhaustive.

13. See Jeff Stein, "The Obamacare Repeal Battle Shows the Power and Limits of Grassroots Organizing," *Vox*, August 10, 2017, https://www.vox.com/policy-and-politics/2017/8/10/16107458/obamacare-repeal-fight-left; Jeff Stein, "The Health Care Resistance Is Working. Just Ask

a Few Republican Senators," *Vox*, July 20, 2017, https://www.vox.com
/policy-and-politics/2017/7/20/16000752/health-resistance-gop-senators.

14. Alexandra Yoon-Hendricks and Zoe Greenberg, "Protests Across U.S.
Call for End to Migrant Family Separations," *New York Times*, July 2, 2018,
https://www.nytimes.com/2018/06/30/us/politics/trump-protests
-family-separation.html.

15. Brent Budowsky, "Trump Resistance Wins Tsunami Elections in 2017,"
The Hill, November 8, 2017, http://thehill.com/opinion/campaign/359344
-trump-resistance-wins-tsunami-elections-in-2017.

16. Christina Capatides, "Badlands National Park Twitter Account Goes
Rogue, Starts Tweeting Scientific Facts," *CBS News*, January 24, 2017,
https://www.cbsnews.com/news/badlands-national-park-twitter-goes
-rogue-starts-tweeting-facts-about-the-environment/.

17. Lourdes A. Vera, Lindsey Dillon, Sara Wylie, and Jennifer Liss Ohayon,
"Data Resistance: A Social Movement Organizational Autoethnog-
raphy of the Environmental Data and Governance Initiative," *Mobilization: An International Quarterly* 23, no. 4 (December 1, 2018): 511–29,
https://doi.org/10.17813/1086-671X-24-4-511; see also Brady Dennis,
"Scientists Are Frantically Copying U.S. Climate Data, Fearing It Might
Vanish Under Trump," *Washington Post*, December 13, 2016, https://www
.washingtonpost.com/news/energy-environment/wp/2016/12/13
/scientists-are-frantically-copying-u-s-climate-data-fearing-it-might
-vanish-under-trump/?utm_term=.485c544ead86.

18. Aja Romano, "The President's Committee on the Arts and Humanities
Resigns, Urging Resistance Against Trump," *Vox*, August 18, 2017,
https://www.vox.com/policy-and-politics/2017/8/18/16169980/arts
-and-humanities-committee-resigns-trump-resist.

19. Amy B. Wang, "Trump's Science Envoy Quits in Scathing Letter with
an Embedded Message: I-M-P-E-A-C-H," *Washington Post*, August 23,
2017, https://www.washingtonpost.com/news/speaking-of-science/wp
/2017/08/23/trumps-science-envoy-quits-with-scathing-letter-with-an
-embedded-message-i-m-p-e-a-c-h/.

20. Robert D. Putnam, *Bowling Alone: The Collapse and Revival of American
Community* (New York: Touchstone, 2000).

21. But see Dana R. Fisher, Dawn M. Dow, and Rashawn Ray, "Intersectionality Takes It to the Streets: Mobilizing Across Diverse Interests for the
Women's March," *Science Advances* 3, no. 9 (September 1, 2017): eaao1390,

https://doi.org/10.1126/sciadv.aao1390; Michael T. Heaney, "Activism in an Era of Partisan Polarization," *PS: Political Science & Politics* 50, no. 4 (October 2017): 1000–1003, https://doi.org/10.1017/S1049096517001159; Meyer and Tarrow, *The Resistance.*

22. For overviews, see Vanessa Williamson and Carly Knight, "Choose Your Own Election Post-Mortem: Part 1," *Brookings* (blog), November 16, 2016, https://www.brookings.edu/blog/fixgov/2016/11/16/choose-your-own-post-mortem-part-1/; Nate Silver, "The Real Story of 2016," *FiveThirtyEight* (blog), January 19, 2017, https://fivethirtyeight.com/features/the-real-story-of-2016/; Zeke J. Miller and Philip Elliott, "Clinton and Trump Aides Clash at Campaign Manager Conference," *Time*, December 2, 2016, http://time.com/4588449/campaign-managers-conference-2016-election/.

23. Dana R. Fisher, *Activism, Inc.: How the Outsourcing of Grassroots Campaigns Is Strangling Progressive Politics in America* (Stanford, Calif: Stanford University Press, 2006).

24. For a review, see Williamson and Knight, "Choose Your Own Election Post-Mortem."

25. See, for example, Drake Baer, "What Is 'Presidential Temperament,' Anyway?," *Science of Us*, August 2, 2016, http://nymag.com/scienceofus/2016/10/what-presidential-temperament-really-is.html; but for a discussion of how Trump was a charismatic candidate, see Tarrow, "Rhythms of Resistance."

26. Fisher, *Activism, Inc.*, 15–16.

27. See discussion in Lester Spence, "Make Sure It Includes Everyone," *Democracy Journal* Spring, no. 44 (April 1, 2017), https://democracyjournal.org/magazine/44/make-sure-it-includes-everyone/.

28. For details, see National Conference of State Legislatures, "State Partisan Composition," http://www.ncsl.org/research/about-state-legislatures/partisan-composition.aspx, accessed October 17, 2017.

29. Tim Dickinson, "Can Democrats Fix the Party?," *Rolling Stone*, June 12, 2017, http://www.rollingstone.com/politics/features/can-democrats-fix-the-party-w487160; see also Michael Tomasky, "The Resistance So Far," *New York Review of Books*, November 9, 2017, http://www.nybooks.com/articles/2017/11/09/the-resistance-so-far/; for a discussion of the 2017 elections, see Matthew Bloch and Jasmine Lee, "Election Results: Murphy Wins New Jersey Governor Race," *New York Times*,

December 20, 2017, https://www.nytimes.com/elections/results/new-jersey-general-elections.

30. Clio Chang, "The Case for Tom Perez Makes No Sense," *The New Republic*, February 23, 2017, https://newrepublic.com/article/140847/case-tom-perez-makes-no-sense.

31. Diana C. Mutz, "Status Threat, Not Economic Hardship, Explains the 2016 Presidential Vote," *Proceedings of the National Academy of Sciences* 115, no. 19 (May 8, 2018): E4330–39, https://doi.org/10.1073/pnas.1718155115.

32. Rory McVeigh and Kevin Estep, *The Politics of Losing: Trump, the Klan, and the Mainstreaming of Resentment* (New York: Columbia University Press, 2019); Daniel Cox, Rachel Lienesch, and Robert P. Jones, "Beyond Economics: Fears of Cultural Displacement Pushed the White Working Class to Trump," *PRRI/The Atlantic Report*, May 9, 2017, https://www.prri.org/research/white-working-class-attitudes-economy-trade-immigration-election-donald-trump/.

33. Jonathan Capehart, "Opinion | Tom Perez on Why the Democratic Party Needs a Dramatic Culture Shift," *Washington Post*, February 14, 2017, https://www.washingtonpost.com/blogs/post-partisan/wp/2017/02/14/tom-perez-on-why-the-democratic-party-needs-a-dramatic-culture-shift/.

34. Gerrymandering and voter suppression have been used to blunt the power of citizens in elections. See Ari Berman, "Yes, the Election Was Rigged. Here's the Proof," *Mother Jones*, December 2017, http://www.motherjones.com/politics/2017/10/voter-suppression-wisconsin-election-2016/; Dana Milbank, "The Election Really Was Rigged," *Washington Post*, November 29, 2016, https://www.washingtonpost.com/opinions/the-election-really-was-rigged/2016/11/29/c2ed58d8-b666-11e6-a677-b608fbb3aaf6_story.html.

35. Marshall Ganz, "Organizing Obama: Campaign, Organizing, Movement," meetings of the American Sociological Association, San Francisco, Calif., 2009, 1; see also Elizabeth McKenna, Hahrie Han, and Jeremy Bird, *Groundbreakers: How Obama's 2.2 Million Volunteers Transformed Campaigning in America* (New York: Oxford University Press, 2015).

36. Matthew Hindman, "Not the Digital Democracy We Ordered," December 9, 2008, http://publius.cc/2008/12/09/not-the-digital-democracy-we-ordered.

37. Ari Melber, "Year One of Organizing for America: The Permanent Field Campaign in a Digital Age," *techPresident Special Report*. January 14, 2010, 4, www.techpresident.com/ofayear1.

38. Ari Berman, *Herding Donkeys: The Fight to Rebuild the Democratic Party and Reshape American Politics* (New York: Picador, 2012), 8; see also Ganz, "Organizing Obama"; McKenna, Han, and Bird, *Groundbreakers*; Micah L. Sifry, "Obama's Lost Army," *The New Republic*, February 9, 2017, https://newrepublic.com/article/140245/obamas-lost -army-inside-fall-grassroots-machine.

39. Dana R. Fisher, "Youth Political Participation: Bridging Activism and Electoral Politics," *Annual Review of Sociology* 38 (2012): 119– 137; McKenna, Han, and Bird, *Groundbreakers*; Berman, *Herding Donkeys*.

40. Theda Skocpol and Vanessa Williamson, *The Tea Party and the Remaking of Republican Conservatism* (New York: Oxford University Press, 2012), x. Organizing for America was renamed Organizing for Action after the 2012 election. For a discussion, see "Grass-Roots Group Born of Obama Campaign Now Helps Push His Causes," *npr.org*, April 15, 2016, http:// www.npr.org/2016/04/15/474303205/grassroots-group-born-of-obama -campaign-now-helps-push-his-causes.

41. Sifry, "Obama's Lost Army"; see also Tim Dickinson, "No We Can't," *Rolling Stone*, February 2, 2010, http://www.rollingstone.com/politics /news/no-we-cant-20100202; Skocpol and Williamson, *The Tea Party and the Remaking of Republican Conservatism*. It is likely that issues raised by Donna Brazile also contributed to the outcome of the 2016 election: see Donna Brazile, *Hacks: The Inside Story of the Break-Ins and Breakdowns That Put Donald Trump in the White House* (New York: Hachette Books, 2017).

42. David Weigel, "Thomas Perez Elected the First Latino Leader of Democratic Party," *Washington Post*, February 25, 2017, https://www .washingtonpost.com/powerpost/tom-perez-elected-as-first-latino -leader-of-democratic-party/2017/02/25/1fd76f52-fad7-11e6-9845 -576c69081518_story.html.

43. Ezra Klein, "Keith Ellison on His DNC Vision, the Democrats' Down-Ballot Collapse, and Identity Politics," *Vox*, January 19, 2017, https://www.vox.com/policy-and-politics/2017/1/19/14322998/keith -ellison-dnc-ezra-klein.

44. Chang, "The Case for Tom Perez Makes No Sense."

45. See, for example, Olivia Beavers, "Longtime DNC Officials Frustrated with Delegate Shake-Up," *The Hill*, October 19, 2017, http://thehill.com/blogs/blog-briefing-room/news/356176-longtime-dnc-officials-ousted-in-shakeup; Brazile, *Hacks*.

46. Tim Dickinson, "How Progressive Activists Are Leading the Trump Resistance," *Rolling Stone*, August 24, 2017, http://www.rollingstone.com/politics/features/how-progressive-activists-are-leading-the-trump-resistance-w499221. It is worth noting that the DNC attempted to join the Resistance with its *Resistance Summer* program, which received a mixed response from activists and groups.

47. Emily Cadei, "The DNC Wants to Join the Resistance. Will Activists Allow It?", *Newsweek*, June 3, 2017, http://www.newsweek.com/dnc-democrats-trump-resistance-620173.

48. "Welcome to Resistance Summer!", *MoveOn.org*, https://act.moveon.org/survey/resistancesummer/, accessed April 20, 2018; "Resistance Summer," *Democratic National Committee*, https://resistsummer.com/, accessed April 20, 2018.

49. Victoria Kaplan, interview with the author, February 20, 2018.

50. Cadei, "The DNC Wants to Join the Resistance."

51. Doug McAdam and Sidney Tarrow, "Ballots and Barricades: On the Reciprocal Relationship Between Elections and Social Movements," *Perspectives on Politics* 8, no. 2 (June 2010): 529–42, https://doi.org/10.1017/S1537592710001234; see also Doug McAdam, Sidney Tarrow, and Charles Tilly, *Dynamics of Contention* (New York: Cambridge University Press, 2001); Fisher, "Youth Political Participation"; Doug McAdam and Karina Kloos, *Deeply Divided: Racial Politics and Social Movements in Postwar America* (New York: Oxford University Press, 2014); Michael T. Heaney and Fabio Rojas, *Party in the Street: The Antiwar Movement and the Democratic Party After 9/11* (New York: Cambridge University Press, 2015).

52. McAdam and Kloos, *Deeply Divided*, 10. This distinction is discussed in detail by McAdam, Tarrow, and Tilly, *Dynamics of Contention*, in which they disaggregate what they call "contained" and "transgressive" forms of contention.

53. Erica Chenoweth and Jeremy Pressman, "This Is What We Learned by Counting the Women's Marches," *Washington Post*, February 7, 2017, https://www.washingtonpost.com/news/monkey-cage/wp/2017/02/07/this-is-what-we-learned-by-counting-the-womens-marches/; see also

Matt Broomfield, "Women's March Against Donald Trump Is the Largest Day of Protests in US History, Say Political Scientists," *The Independent*, January 23, 2017, https://www.independent.co.uk/news/world/americas/womens-march-anti-donald-trump-womens-rights-largest-protest-demonstration-us-history-political-a7541081.html; Marie Berry and Erica Chenoweth, "Who Made the Women's March?", in David S. Meyer and Sidney Tarrow, eds., *The Resistance: The Dawn of the Anti-Trump Opposition Movement* (New York: Oxford University Press, 2018), 187–206.

54. I want to thank an anonymous reviewer of the manuscript for highlighting this point.

55. "Letting Members Lead: The Mess and Magic of Distributed Organizing," *Netroots Nation*, July 15, 2016, panel discussion, https://www.netroots nation.org/nn_events/nn-16/letting-members-lead-the-mess-and -magic-of-distributed-organizing/. For details on the way civil society uses these digital tools, see Clay Shirky, "The Political Power of Social Media," *Foreign Affairs*, December 20, 2010, https://www.foreignaffairs .com/articles/2010-12-20/political-power-social-media; Zeynep Tufekci, *Twitter and Tear Gas: The Power and Fragility of Networked Protest* (New Haven, Conn.: Yale University Press, 2017).

56. Becky Bond and Zack Exley, *Rules for Revolutionaries: How Big Organizing Can Change Everything* (White River Junction, Vt.: Chelsea Green, 2016), 4.

57. For more on new digital tools, see David Karpf, *The MoveOn Effect: The Unexpected Transformation of American Political Advocacy* (New York: Oxford University Press, 2012), chap. 5; for more international perspectives, see Shirky, "The Political Power of Social Media"; Tufekci, *Twitter and Tear Gas*; for more on distributed organizing, see Dominik Böhler, *On the Nature of Distributed Organizing*, Market—Und Unternehmensentwicklung Markets and Organisations (Wiesbaden, Germany: Gabler Verlag, 2014), //www.springer.com/la/book/9783658061227; Bond and Exley, *Rules for Revolutionaries*.

58. During the two years I was doing research for this project, I signed up for many events, and only once did I sign up on an actual paper list (and that was after signing up online first).

59. Karpf, *The MoveOn Effect*, xii–xiii.

60. Theda Skocpol, *Diminished Democracy: From Membership to Management in American Civic Life* (Norman: University of Oklahoma Press, 2013),

18. 139; see also Theda Skocpol, Marshall Ganz, and Ziad Munson, "A Nation of Organizers: The Institutional Origins of Civic Voluntarism in the United States," *The American Political Science Review* 94, no. 3 (2000): 527–46, https://doi.org/10.2307/2585829; Hahrie Han, "The Organizational Roots of Political Activism: Field Experiments on Creating a Relational Context," *American Political Science Review* 110, no. 2 (May 2016): 296–307, https://doi.org/10.1017/S000305541600006X.

61. For thoughts on the potential based on the 2016 Sanders campaign, see Bond and Exley, *Rules for Revolutionaries*.

62. For an overview, see David Karpf, *Analytic Activism: Digital Listening and the New Political Strategy* (New York: Oxford University Press, 2016); David Karpf, "Analytic Activism and Its Limitations," *Social Media + Society* 4, no. 1 (January 1, 2018): 2056305117750718, https://doi.org/10.1177/2056305117750718; Tufekci, *Twitter and Tear Gas*. For a discussion of collective identity formation through digital tools, see Deana A. Rohlinger and Leslie A. Bunnage, "Collective Identity in the Digital Age: Thin and Thick Identities in Moveon.Org and the Tea Party Movement," *Mobilization: An International Quarterly* 23, no. 2 (June 1, 2018): 135–57, https://doi.org/10.17813/1086-671X-23-2-135; see also Jennifer Earl and Katrina Kimport, *Digitally Enabled Social Change: Activism in the Internet Age* (Cambridge, Mass.: MIT Press, 2013).

63. Dana R Fisher, Dawn M. Dow, and Rashawn Ray, "The Demographics of the #Resistance," *Salon*, June 3, 2017, https://www.salon.com/2017/06/03/the-demographics-of-the-resistance_partner/; Eric Liu, "How Donald Trump Is Reviving American Democracy," *The Atlantic*, March 8, 2017, https://www.theatlantic.com/politics/archive/2017/03/how-donald-trump-is-reviving-our-democracy/518928/.

64. Skocpol and Williamson, *The Tea Party and the Remaking of Republican Conservatism*.

65. Robert N. Bellah, Richard Madsen, William M. Sullivan, Ann Swidler, and Steven M. Tipton, *Habits of the Heart: Individualism and Commitment in American Life: Updated Edition with a New Introduction* (Berkeley: University of California Press, 1996); Putnam, *Bowling Alone*; Skocpol, *Diminished Democracy*.

66. See, particularly, Alexis de Tocqueville, *Democracy in America* (New Rochelle, N.Y.: Arlington House, 1966); Gabriel Abraham Almond and Sidney Verba, *The Civic Culture: Political Attitudes and Democracy in Five Nations* (Princeton, N.J.: Princeton University Press, 1963). For

more recent comparisons, see Everett Carll Ladd, *The Ladd Report* (New York: Free Press, 1999); Evan Schofer and Marion Fourcade-Gourinchas, "The Structural Contexts of Civic Engagement: Voluntary Association Membership in Comparative Perspective," *American Sociological Review* 66 (2001): 806–2; Evan Schofer and Wesley Longhofer, "The Structural Sources of Association," *American Journal of Sociology* 117, no. 2 (2011): 539–85.

67. Yongren Shi, Fedor A. Dokshin, Michael Genkin, and Matthew E. Brashears, "A Member Saved Is a Member Earned? The Recruitment -Retention Trade-Off and Organizational Strategies for Membership Growth," *American Sociological Review* 82, no. 2 (April 1, 2017): 407–34, https://doi.org/10.1177/0003122417693616; Doug McAdam and Ronnelle Paulsen, "Specifying the Relationship Between Social Ties and Activism," *American Journal of Sociology* 99, no. 3 (1993): 640–67; Han, "The Organizational Roots of Political Activism"; Sidney Verba, Kay Lehman Schlozman, and Henry E. Brady, *Voice and Equality: Civic Voluntarism in American Politics* (Cambridge, Mass.: Harvard University Press, 1995).

68. Mario Luis Small, *Someone to Talk To* (New York: Oxford University Press, 2017); for a discussion of diversity and social capital, see Maria Abascal and Delia Baldassarri, "Love Thy Neighbor? Ethnoracial Diversity and Trust Reexamined," *American Journal of Sociology* 121, no. 3 (2015): 722–82, https://doi.org/10.1086/683144.

69. Putnam, *Bowling Alone*; Miller McPherson, Lynn Smith-Lovin, and Matthew E. Brashears, "Social Isolation in America: Changes in Core Discussion Networks over Two Decades," *American Sociological Review* 71, no. 3 (June 1, 2006): 353–75, https://doi.org/10.1177/000312240607100301; Robert N. Bellah, Richard Madsen, William M. Sullivan, Ann Swidler, and Steven M. Tipton, *Habits of the Heart: Individualism and Commitment in American Life* (Berkeley: University of California Press, 2007).

70. James M. Jasper and Jane D. Poulsen, "Recruiting Strangers and Friends: Moral Shocks and Social Networks in Animal Rights and Anti-Nuclear Protests," *Social Problems* 42, no. 4 (1995): 498, https://doi.org/10.2307/3097043; see also James M. Jasper, *The Art of Moral Protest: Culture, Biography, and Creativity in Social Movements* (Chicago: University of Chicago Press, 1997); for a discussion of grievances and threats, see Rachel G. McKane and Holly J. McCammon, "Why We March: The Role of Grievances, Threats, and Movement Organizational

Resources in the 2017 Women's Marches," *Mobilization: An International Quarterly* 23, no. 4 (December 1, 2018): 401–24, https://doi.org/10.17813/1086-671X-23-4-401.

71. For a discussion on undoing the Obama legacy, see Michael Grunwald, "Trump's Secret Weapon Against Obama's Legacy," *Politico*, April 10, 2017, https://www.politico.com/magazine/story/2017/04/donald-trump-obama-legacy-215009. For a discussion on Trump's executive orders, see Michael C. Dorf and Michael S. Chu, "Lawyers as Activists," in *The Resistance: The Dawn of the Anti-Trump Opposition Movement*, ed. David S. Meyer and Sidney Tarrow (New York: Oxford University Press, 2018), 127–42.

72. Jeffrey M. Berry and Sarah Sobieraj, *The Outrage Industry: Political Opinion Media and the New Incivility* (New York: Oxford University Press, 2014), 5.

73. Donald J. Trump, *Twitter*, October 22, 2018, https://twitter.com/realDonaldTrump/status/1054351078328885248.

74. Stephen Collinson, "Trump Shocks with Racist New Ad Days Before Midterms," *CNN Politics*, November 1, 2018, https://www.cnn.com/2018/10/31/politics/donald-trump-immigration-paul-ryan-midterms/index.html.

75. Citizens United v. Federal Election Comm'n 558 U.S. 310 (2010), https://supreme.justia.com/cases/federal/us/558/310/. For more on tax-exempt social welfare groups and super PACs, see "Dark Money," *OpenSecrets.org*, https://www.opensecrets.org/dark-money/dark-money-basics.php; Philip Bump, "How Citizens United Is—and Isn't—to Blame for the Dark Money President Obama Hates So Much," *Washington Post*, January 21, 2015, https://www.washingtonpost.com/news/the-fix/wp/2015/01/21/how-citizens-united-is-and-isnt-to-blame-for-the-dark-money-president-obama-hates-so-much/.

76. Editorial Board, "Dark Money Helped Win the Senate," *New York Times*, November 8, 2014, http://www.nytimes.com/2014/11/09/opinion/sunday/dark-money-helped-win-the-senate.html?_r=0.

77. Jane Mayer, *Dark Money: The Hidden History of the Billionaires Behind the Rise of the Radical Right* (New York: Doubleday, 2016), http://www.penguinrandomhouse.com/books/215462/dark-money-by-jane-mayer/9780385535595/.

78. This list is not meant to be exhaustive.

79. Elena Schneider, "Koch-Backed Group Targets First GOP Incumbent in Primary," *Politico*, May 12, 2016, https://www.politico.com/story/2016/05/koch-group-targets-renee-ellmers-223124.

80. " 'Dark Money': Koch Brothers Donations Push Their Political Agenda," *npr.org*, interview of Jane Mayer by Steve Inskeep, http://www.npr.org/2016/01/19/463551038/dark-money-delves-into-how-koch-brothers-donations-push-their-political-agenda.

81. Vanessa Williamson, Theda Skocpol, and John Coggin, "The Tea Party and the Remaking of Republican Conservatism," *Perspectives on Politics* 9, no. 1 (2011): 25–43, at 29.

82. "Outside Spending," *OpenSecrets*, 2016, http://www.opensecrets.org/outsidespending/summ.php?cycle=2016&disp=D&type=V&superonly=N.

83. Darren Samuelsohn, "Inside Clinton's Plan to Win Over Millenials," *Politico*, June 20, 2016, http://www.politico.com/story/2016/06/hillary-clinton-millennials-young-voters-224507. NextGen Climate became NextGen America

84. Katy Steinmetz, "This California Billionaire Is Spending Millions to Impeach Trump," *Time*, October 27, 2017, http://time.com/5001180/donald-trump-impeachment-tom-steyer/.

85. See, particularly, Aldon D. Morris, *The Origins of the Civil Rights Movement: Black Communities Organizing for Change* (New York: Free Press, 1986); Doug McAdam, *Political Process and the Development of Black Insurgency, 1930–1970*, 2nd ed. (Chicago: University of Chicago Press, 1982).

86. Personal communication with author, September 27, 2017.

87. For a full discussion, see Suzanne Staggenborg, "The Consequences of Professionalization and Formalization in the Pro-Choice Movement," *American Sociological Review* 53, no. 4 (1988): 585–605, https://doi.org/10.2307/2095851.

88. For a full list of cosponsors for the Women's March, see https://www.womensmarch.com/partners, accessed October 18, 2017.

89. For a discussion of the tensions within the Resistance, see Kenneth P. Vogel, "The 'Resistance,' Raising Big Money, Upends Liberal Politics," *New York Times*, October 7, 2017, https://www.nytimes.com/2017/10/07/us/politics/democrats-resistance-fundraising.html.

90. Meyer and Tarrow, *The Resistance: The Dawn of the Anti-Trump Opposition Movement*.

91. The full text of *Indivisible: A Practical Guide for Resisting the Trump Agenda* is available for download at https://indivisible.org/campaign/indivisible-guide, accessed April 19, 2019.

92. Sarah Dohl, chief communications officer of Indivisible, interview with author, January 16, 2018.

93. For details see "Coordinate with other Indivisible groups!", *Indivisible*, https://indivisible.org/coordinate-other-indivisible-groups, accessed November 30, 2018.

2. RESISTANCE IN THE STREETS

1. My dissertation became my first book: Dana R. Fisher, *National Governance and the Global Climate Change Regime* (Lanham, Md.: Rowman & Littlefield, 2004).

2. For an overview of the insider/outsider model, see William A. Maloney, Grant Jordan, and Andrew M. McLaughlin, "Interest Groups and Public Policy: The Insider/Outsider Model Revisited," *Journal of Public Policy* 14, no. 1 (1994): 17–38.

3. For an overview, see Francesca Polletta and James M. Jasper, "Collective Identity and Social Movements," *Annual Review of Sociology* 27, no. 1 (2001): 283–305, https://doi.org/10.1146/annurev.soc.27.1.283.

4. For a full discussion of what I found, see Dana R. Fisher, Kevin Stanley, David Berman, and Gina Neff, "How Do Organizations Matter? Mobilization and Support for Participants at Five Globalization Protests," *Social Problems* 52, no. 1 (February 2005): 102–21, https://doi.org/10.1525/sp.2005.52.1.102.

5. For the full story, see Perry Stein and Sandhya Somashekhar, "It Started with a Retiree. Now the Women's March Could Be the Biggest Inauguration Demonstration," *Washington Post*, January 3, 2017, https://www.washingtonpost.com/national/it-started-with-a-grandmother-in-hawaii-now-the-womens-march-on-washington-is-poised-to-be-the-biggest-inauguration-demonstration/2017/01/03/8af61686-c6e2-11e6-bf4b-2c06 4d32a4bf_story.html.

6. The survey instrument we used on January 21, 2017, is available at http://drfisher.umd.edu/WomensMarchSurvey.pdf.

7. For a discussion of Occupy Wall Street events, see David B. Grusky, Doug McAdam, Rob Reich, and Debra Satz, eds., *Occupy the Future* (Cambridge, Mass.: MIT Press, 2013); for a discussion of the roots of the Resistance, see David S. Meyer and Sidney Tarrow, *The Resistance: The Dawn of the Anti-Trump Opposition Movement* (New York: Oxford University Press, 2018), chap. 1.

8. Erica Chenoweth and Jeremy Pressman, "This Is What We Learned by Counting the Women's Marches," *Washington Post*, February 7, 2017, https://www.washingtonpost.com/news/monkey-cage/wp/2017/02/07/this-is-what-we-learned-by-counting-the-womens-marches/.

9. Meyer and Tarrow, *The Resistance.*

10. See the methodological appendix for details about specific marches at which data were collected. For an overview, see Dana R. Fisher, Kenneth T.Andrews , Neal Caren, Erica Chenoweth, Michael T. Heaney, Tommy Leung, Nathan Perkins, and Jeremy Pressman. 2019. "The Science of Contemporary Street Protest: New Efforts in the United States." *Science Advances.*

11. For a summary of the methodology, see Fisher, Stanley, Berman, and Neff, "How Do Organizations Matter?"; Dana R. Fisher, Dawn M. Dow, and Rashawn Ray, "Intersectionality Takes It to the Streets: Mobilizing Across Diverse Interests for the Women's March," *Science Advances* 3, no. 9 (September 1, 2017): eaao1390, https://doi.org/10.1126/sciadv.aao1390.

12. Kenneth T. Andrews, Neal Caren, and Alyssa Browne, "Protesting Trump," *Mobilization: An International Quarterly* 23, no. 4 (December 2018): 393–400, https://doi.org/10.17813/1086-671X-23-4-393; Kraig Beyerlein, Peter Ryan, Aliyah Abu-Hazeem, and Amity Pauley, "The 2017 Women's March: A National Study of Solidarity Events," *Mobilization: An International Quarterly* 23, no. 4 (December 2018): 425–49, https://doi.org/10.17813/1086-671X-23-4-425.

13. Graham St. John, "Protestival: Global Days of Action and Carnivalized Politics in the Present," *Social Movement Studies* 7, no. 2 (2008): 167–90.

14. For details on organizing events, see Becky Bond and Zack Exley, *Rules for Revolutionaries: How Big Organizing Can Change Everything* (White River Junction, Vt.: Chelsea Green, 2016), chap. 6; for information on coordinating through conference calls and huddles, see Lahitou, Jessicah. 2017. "How To Host A Women's March Huddle." Bustle. February 3. Retrieved May 21, 2019 (https://www.bustle.com/p/how-to-host-a-womens-march-huddle-because-action-2-is-keeping-the-momentum-alive-35280).

15. For more on the Hawaiian grandmother, see Stein and Somashekhar, "It Started with a Retiree"; for a discussion of the day of action, see Chenoweth and Pressman, "This Is What We Learned by Counting the Women's Marches."

16. See *Pussyhat Project*, https://www.pussyhatproject.com/, accessed May 21, 2019.

17. Ben Guarino, "The March for Science Began with This Person's 'Throw-away Line' on Reddit," *Washington Post*, April 21, 2017, https://www.washingtonpost.com/news/speaking-of-science/wp/2017/04/21/the-march-for-science-began-with-this-persons-throwaway-line-on-reddit/; for more on the march, see *March for Science*, May 4, 2019, https://www.marchforscience.com/our-mission.

18. For a full list, see "Our Partners," *March for Science*, https://www.marchforscience.com/partners, accessed June 20, 2018.

19. See, for example, Nicholas St. Fleur, "Scientists, Feeling Under Siege, March Against Trump Policies," *New York Times*, April 22, 2017, https://www.nytimes.com/2017/04/22/science/march-for-science.html; Mark Lynas, "Scientists to Take to the Streets in Global March for Truth," *The Guardian*, April 18, 2017, http://www.theguardian.com/environment/2017/apr/18/scientists-take-streets-global-march-truth; Kate Sheridan, "March for Science: Who Is Going to Attend the Event?", *STAT*, April 19, 2017, https://www.statnews.com/2017/04/19/who-attends-march-for-science/; for a discussion of the polarizing effects of the March for Science, see Matthew Motta, "The Polarizing Effect of the March for Science on Attitudes Toward Scientists," *PS: Political Science & Politics* 51, no. 4 (2018): 782–88.

20. Dana R. Fisher, "Scientists in the Resistance," *Sociological Forum* 33, no. 1 (December 2017): 247–50, https://doi.org/10.1111/socf.12396; but see Dana R. Fisher and Scott Frickel, "Will Scientists Gear Up for Activism in the Age of Trump?", *The American Prospect*, July 12, 2018, http://prospect.org/article/will-scientists-gear-activism-age-trump.

21. Laura Smith-Spark and Jason Hanna, "March for Science: Protesters Gather Worldwide to Support 'Evidence'," *CNN*, April 22, 2017, https://www.cnn.com/2017/04/22/health/global-march-for-science/index.html.

22. Nicholas Fandos, "Climate March Draws Thousands of Protesters Alarmed by Trump's Environmental Agenda," *New York Times*, April 29, 2017, https://www.nytimes.com/2017/04/29/us/politics/peoples-climate-march-trump.html.

23. Chris Mooney, Joe Heim, and Brady Dennis, "Climate March Draws Massive Crowd to D.C. in Sweltering Heat," *Washington Post*, April 29, 2017, https://www.washingtonpost.com/national/health-science/climate-march-expected-to-draw-massive-crowd-to-dc-in-sweltering-heat/2017/04/28/1bdf5e66-2c3a-11e7-b605-33413c691853_story.html?utm_term=.dc524c3be270.

24. Robinson Meyer, "The Climate March's Big Tent Strategy Draws a Big Crowd," *The Atlantic*, April 30, 2017, https://www.theatlantic .com/science/archive/2017/04/the-people-who-came-to-the-climate -march/524865/; Mooney, Heim, and Dennis, "Climate March Draws Massive Crowd to D.C. in Sweltering Heat."

25. Perry Stein, "March for Racial Justice and March for Black Women Will Converge in D.C. This Weekend," *Washington Post*, September 28, 2017, https://www.washingtonpost.com/local/march-for-racial-justice -and-march-for-black-women-will-converge-in-dc-this-weekend /2017/09/28/8c5bd2e8-a45b-11e7-b14f-f41773cd5a14_story.html; for a discussion of these protests and their "tactical neutralization," see Sharon Erickson Nepstad and Alexis M. Kenney, "Legitimation Battles, Backfire Dynamics, and Tactical Persistence in the NFL Anthem Protests, 2016–2017," *Mobilization: An International Quarterly* 23, no. 4 (December 2018): 469–83, https://doi.org/10.17813/1086-671X-23-4-469.

26. Rachel Chason, "'Let the Black Women Lead': Marches Converge on D.C. to Highlight Racial Injustice," *Washington Post*, September 30, 2017, https://www.washingtonpost.com/local/let-the-black-women-lead -marches-converge-on-dc-to-highlight-racial-injustice/2017/09/30 /aa213ecc-a612-11e7-b14f-f41773cd5a14_story.html; Emily Baumgaertner, "Marches for Racial Justice and Black Women Converge in Washington," *New York Times*, September 30, 2017, https://www.nytimes. com/2017/09/30/us/politics/washington-dc-racism-protests.html.

27. For more on the Las Vegas rally, see Rebecca Savransky, "Women's March Organizers to Launch Voter Registration Tour," *The Hill*, January 17, 2018, http://thehill.com/blogs/blog-briefing-room/news/369294-womens -march-organizers-to-mark-one-year-anniversary-by-kicking; for a discussion of the 2018 march, see Farah Stockman, "One Year After Women's March, More Activism but Less Unity," *New York Times*, January 15, 2018, shttps://www.nytimes.com/2018/01/15/us/womens-march-anniversary.html.

28. See Erica Chenoweth and Jeremy Pressman, "January's Women's March Brought Out More Than a Million People—and Many More Also Protested During the Month," *Washington Post*, February 26, 2018, https://www.washingtonpost.com/news/monkey-cage/wp/2018/02/26 /januarys-womens-march-brought-out-more-than-a-million-people -and-many-more-also-protested-during-the-month/?utm_term =.a17c2c08cd2c; Erica Chenoweth and Jeremy Pressman, "The Women's March Could Change Politics Like the Tea Party Did," *The Guardian*,

January 31, 2018, https://www.theguardian.com/commentisfree/2018/jan/31/womens-march-politics-tea-party.

29. For details on March Forward Virginia, see "Women's March on Washington 2018," https://www.marchdc.com/qa/, accessed August 17, 2018; see also Michael Alison Chandler and Joe Heim, "Protesters Gather for a Second Women's March in Nation's Capital," *Washington Post*, January 20, 2018, https://www.washingtonpost.com/local/protesters-gather-for-a-second-womens-march-in-nations-capital/2018/01/20/c641bf16-fdef-11e7-ad8c-ecbb62019393_story.html.

30. For details on celebrities, see Lisa Ryan, "All the Celebrities Attending the March For Our Lives," *The Cut*, March 23, 2018, https://www.thecut.com/2018/03/march-for-our-lives-celebrities-performers-speakers.html; for discussion on the day's events, see Erica Bond, Erica Chenoweth, and Jeremy Pressman, "Did You Attend the March for Our Lives? Here's What It Looked Like Nationwide," *Washington Post*, April 13, 2018, https://www.washingtonpost.com/news/monkey-cage/wp/2018/04/13/did-you-attend-the-march-for-our-lives-heres-what-it-looked-like-nationwide/; for a discussion of turnout in Washington, D.C., see Dana R Fisher, "Here's Who Actually Attended the March For Our Lives. (No, It Wasn't Mostly Young People)," *Washington Post*, March 28, 2018, https://www.washingtonpost.com/news/monkey-cage/wp/2018/03/28/heres-who-actually-attended-the-march-for-our-lives-no-it-wasnt-mostly-young-people/?utm_term=.55892becf76c.

31. For a list of organizations supporting this effort, see "Families Belong Together—Partners," *MoveOn,* https://act.moveon.org/survey/families-belong-together-partners/, accessed August 20, 2018.

32. Erica Chenoweth and Jeremy Pressman, "Millions of Protesters Turned Out in June—More Than in Any Month Since Trump's Inauguration," *Washington Post*, August 31, 2018, https://www.washingtonpost.com/amphtml/news/monkey-cage/wp/2018/08/31/millions-of-protesters-turned-out-in-june-more-than-in-any-month-since-trumps-inauguration/?utm_term=.59bdc4fa4014&__twitter_impression=true; for discussion of discrepancies in the number of events, see Fisher et al., "The Science of Protest."

33. For a discussion of turnout at this event, see Dana R. Fisher, "Who Came Out in the Brutal Heat to the 'Families Belong Together' March? Here's Our Data," *Washington Post*, July 3, 2018, https://www.washingtonpost.com/news/monkey-cage/wp/2018/07/03/who-came-out-in-the-brutal-heat-to-the-families-belong-together-march-heres-our-data/.

34. Lara Putnam and Theda Skocpol, "Middle America Reboots Democracy," *Democracy Journal*, February 20, 2018, https://democracyjournal.org /arguments/middle-america-reboots-democracy/; see also Judith Shulevitz, "Year One: Resistance Research," *New York Review of Books* (blog), November 9, 2017, http://www.nybooks.com/daily/2017/11/09/year-one -resistance-research/.

35. Doug McAdam, *Political Process and the Development of Black Insurgency, 1930–1970*, 2nd ed. (Chicago: University of Chicago Press, 1982); Alan Schussman and Sarah Anne Soule, "Process and Protest: Accounting for Individual Protest Participation," *Social Forces* 84, no. 2 (2005): 1083–1108, https://doi.org/10.1353/sof.2006.0034.

36. See census data at https://www.census.gov/content/dam/Census/library /publications/2016/demo/p20-578.pdf.

37. For details, see Fisher and Frickel, "Will Scientists Gear Up for Activism in the Age of Trump?"

38. Sarah Ruiz-Grossman, "Millennials Are the Foot Soldiers of the Resistance," *Huffington Post*, February 23, 2017, https://www.huffingtonpost .com/entry/trump-protest-poll_us_58addc16e4b0d0a6ef47517e.

39. Average ages are based on mean scores. It is important to remember that our Institutional Review Board protocol required that we collect data only from participants over the age of eighteen.

40. Nancy Whittier, "Generational Spillover in the Resistance to Trump," in *The Resistance: The Dawn of the Anti-Trump Opposition Movement*, ed. David S. Meyer and Sidney Tarrow (New York: Oxford University Press, 2018), 207–29.

41. Based on calculations from data available at https://www.census.gov /prod/2012pubs/acsbr10-19.pdf, accessed May 9, 2017.

42. Respondents were asked to place themselves on a 7-point scale from very Left to very Right.

43. Fisher, "Here's Who Actually Attended the March For Our Lives."

44. Joris Verhulst and Stefaan Walgrave, "The First Time Is the Hardest? A Cross-National and Cross-Issue Comparison of First-Time Protest Participants," *Political Behavior* 31, no. 3 (September 2009): 455–84, https://doi .org/10.1007/s11109-008-9083-8; see also Clare Saunders, Maria Grasso, Cristiana Olcese, Emily Rainsford, and Christopher Rootes, "Explaining Differential Protest Participation: Novices, Returners, Repeaters, and Stalwarts," *Mobilization: An International Quarterly* 17, no. 3 (September 2012): 263–80, https://doi.org/10.17813/maiq.17.3.bqm553573058t478.

45. For a discussion of the higher percentage at the March for Our Lives, see Fisher, "Here's Who Actually Attended the March for Our Lives. (No, It Wasn't Mostly Young People.)."

46. Sidney Tarrow, "Rhythms of Resistance: The Anti-Trumpian Movement in a Cycle of Contention," in *The Resistance: The Dawn of the Anti-Trump Opposition Movement,* ed. David S. Meyer and Sidney Tarrow (New York: Oxford University Press, 2018), 187–206; see also Dana R. Fisher and Lorien Jasny, "Understanding Persistence in the Resistance," *Sociological Forum,* 2019, https://doi.org/10.31235/osf.io /y367j.

47. For a comparison to the general population, see R. J. Reinhart, "One in Three Americans Have Felt Urge to Protest," *Gallup News,* August 24, 2018, https://news.gallup.com/poll/241634/one-three-americans-felt-urge -protest.aspx?utm_source=alert&utm_medium=email&utm_content =morelink&utm_campaign=syndication.

48. See, particularly, Saunders, Grasso, Olcese, Rainsford, and Rootes, "Explaining Differential Protest Participation"; Verhulst and Walgrave, "The First Time Is the Hardest?"; for extensive analysis of these data, see Fisher and Jasny, "Understanding Persistence in the Resistance."

49. But see Michael T. Heaney and Fabio Rojas, *Party in the Street: The Antiwar Movement and the Democratic Party After 9/11* (New York: Cambridge University Press, 2015); Wooseok Jung, Brayden G. King, and Sarah A. Soule, "Issue Bricolage: Explaining the Configuration of the Social Movement Sector, 1960–1995," *American Journal of Sociology* 120, no. 1 (July 2014): 187–225; Dan J. Wang and Sarah A. Soule, "Tactical Innovation in Social Movements: The Effects of Peripheral and Multi-Issue Protest," *American Sociological Review* 81, no. 3 (June 2016): 517–48, https://doi.org/10.1177/0003122416644414.

50. For discussion of the United States as a "national of joiners," see Arthur M. Schlesinger, "Biography of a Nation of Joiners," *The American Historical Review* 50, no. 1 (1944): 1–25, https://doi.org/10.2307/1843565.

51. Respondents could list any number of issues. For details on how these data were coded and analyzed, see Fisher, Dow, and Ray, "Intersectionality Takes It to the Streets." Participants at subsequent marches were given a checklist of potential motivations. For details, see Dana R. Fisher, Lorien Jasny, and Dawn M. Dow, "Why Are We Here? Patterns of Intersectional Motivations Across the Resistance," *Mobilization: An International Quarterly* 23, no. 4 (December 2018): 451–68.

52. For an overview, see Kimberlé Williams Crenshaw, "Mapping the Margins: Intersectionality, Identity Politics, and Violence Against Women of Color," *Stanford Law Review* 43, no. 6 (1991): 1241–99, https://doi.org/10.2307/1229039; Patricia Hill Collins, *Black Feminist Thought: Knowledge, Consciousness, and the Politics of Empowerment* (New York: Routledge, 2002).

53. Wendy Brown, *States of Injury: Power and Freedom in Late Modernity* (Princeton, N.J.: Princeton University Press, 1995); Nancy Ehrenreich, "Subordination and Symbiosis: Mechanisms of Mutual Support Between Subordinating Systems," *UMKC Law Review* 71 (2002): 251.

54. See, particularly, Anna Carastathis, "Identity Categories as Potential Coalitions," *Signs* 38, no. 4 (2013): 941–65, https://doi.org/10.1086/669573; Dorothy Roberts and Sujatha Jesudason, "Moverment Intersectionality: The Case of Race, Gender, Disability, and Genetic Technologies," *Du Bois Review: Social Science Research on Race* 10, no. 2 (October 2013): 313–28, https://doi.org/10.1017/S1742058X13000210; Nancy D. Wadsworth, "Intersectionality in California's Same-Sex Marriage Battles: A Complex Proposition," *Political Research Quarterly* 64, no. 1 (2011): 200–216; see also Erin M. Adam, "Intersectional Coalitions: The Paradoxes of Rights-Based Movement Building in LGBTQ and Immigrant Communities," *Law & Society Review* 51, no. 1 (March 2017): 132–67, https://doi.org/10.1111/lasr.12248.

55. See, particularly, Crenshaw, "Mapping the Margins"; see also Wadsworth, "Intersectionality in California's Same-Sex Marriage Battles"; Veronica Terriquez, "Intersectional Mobilization, Social Movement Spillover, and Queer Youth Leadership in the Immigrant Rights Movement," *Social Problems* 62, no. 3 (August 2015): 343–62, https://doi.org/10.1093/socpro/spv010.

56. The difference between writing in motivations on a paper survey and checking off issues on an electronic survey on a tablet may have contributed to the increase in number of issues mentioned. For details, see Fisher, Jasny, and Dow, "Why Are We Here?"

57. This uptick may be due in part to changes in the survey instrument. For more details, see methodological appendix.

58. For more details, see Fisher, "Here's Who Actually Attended the March For Our Lives."

59. For a discussion of how this event was unique, see Fisher, "Who Came Out in the Brutal Heat to the 'Families Belong Together' March?"

60. Fisher, Dow, and Ray, "Intersectionality Takes It to the Streets," 1.
61. Fisher, Jasny, and Dow, "Why Are We Here?"
62. For a full discussion of moral shocks, see James M. Jasper and Jane D. Poulsen, "Recruiting Strangers and Friends: Moral Shocks and Social Networks in Animal Rights and Anti-Nuclear Protests," *Social Problems* 42, no. 4 (1995): 493–512, https://doi.org/10.2307/3097043.
63. For an overview of tactics used by activists, see Kathleen M. Blee, *Democracy in the Making: How Activist Groups Form* (Oxford: Oxford University Press, 2014), chap. 1.
64. Aldon D. Morris, *The Origins of the Civil Rights Movement: Black Communities Organizing for Change* (New York: Free Press, 1986).
65. Personal correspondence with author 26 September 2017.
66. For a discussion about who is persisting in the Resistance, see Fisher and Jasny, "Understanding Persistence in the Resistance."
67. Chris Aalcantara, Sahil Chinoy, and Ted Mellnik, "Is Your U.S. Representative Holding a Town Hall in August? Probably Not," *Washington Post*, August 19, 2017, https://www.washingtonpost.com/graphics/2017/politics/summer-recess-town-halls/.
68. Fisher and Jasny, "Understanding Persistence in the Resistance."
69. Fisher, Dow, and Ray, "Intersectionality Takes It to the Streets"; Meyer and Tarrow, *The Resistance*; Putnam and Skocpol, "Middle America Reboots Democracy."
70. See also Meyer and Tarrow, *The Resistance*.

3. ORGANIZING THE RESISTANCE IN THE DISTRICTS

1. Sophie Tatum, "More than 300 Protesters Arrested as Kavanaugh Demonstrations Pack Capitol Hill," *CNN*, October 5, 2018, https://www.cnn.com/2018/10/04/politics/kavanaugh-protests-us-capitol/index.html.
2. Although the media reported instances of supporters of Justice Kavanaugh visiting Senate members' offices, I personally did not see any during my time on the Hill that week. Because they were not following instructions to dress in identifiable outfits, they were not as visible as the opposition.
3. For details, see Martine Powers, "The Senate Subway: The New Epicenter of American Democracy?", *Washington Post*, August 15, 2017,

https://www.washingtonpost.com/local/trafficandcommuting/the
-senate-subway-the-new-epicenter-of-american-democracy/2017
/08/15/312ed3aa-7609-11e7-8f39-eeb7d3a2d304_story.html?utm_term
=.8e9c21303b82.

4. See, for example, Sidney Verba, Kay Lehman Schlozman, and Henry
E. Brady, *Voice and Equality: Civic Voluntarism in American Politics*
(Cambridge, Mass.: Harvard University Press, 1995).

5. Data extracted from the most recent General Social Survey is available
at https://gssdataexplorer.norc.org/projects, accessed April 12, 2018.

6. Pew Research Center, "As Midterms Near, Democrats Are More
Politically Active Than Republicans," August 16, 2018, http://www
.people-press.org/2018/08/16/as-midterms-near-democrats-are-more
-politically-active-than-republicans/; for some historical context, see
Russell J. Dalton, *The Good Citizen: How a Younger Generation Is Reshaping American Politics* (Washington, D.C.: CQ Press, 2015).

7. Mary Jordan and Scott Clement, "Echoes of Vietnam: Millions of
Americans Are Taking to the Streets," *Washington Post*, April 6, 2018,
https://www.washingtonpost.com/news/national/wp/2018/04/06
/feature/in-reaction-to-trump-millions-of-americans-are-joining-protests
-and-getting-political/.

8. Neal Caren, Raj Andrew Ghoshal, and Vanesa Ribas, "A Social
Movement Generation: Cohort and Period Trends in Protest Attendance and Petition Signing," *American Sociological Review* 76, no. 1
(February 2011): 127, https://doi.org/10.1177/0003122410395369; for a
broader discussion of lifestyle politics, see W. Lance Bennett, "The
UnCivic Culture: Communication, Identity, and the Rise of Lifestyle
Politics," *PS: Political Science and Politics* 31, no. 4 (December 1998):
741–61, https://doi.org/10.1017/S1049096500053270.

9. Although connection to organizations varied from protest to protest,
across all events, the percentage of protest participants who reported hearing about the event from an organization was lower than the 41 percent
found in my research of the globalization movement. For details, see
Dana R. Fisher, Kevin Stanley, David Berman, and Gina Neff, "How
Do Organizations Matter? Mobilization and Support for Participants
at Five Globalization Protests," *Social Problems* 52, no. 1 (February 2005):
102–21, https://doi.org/10.1525/sp.2005.52.1.102.

10. For example, the role of Facebook in turning out people at different
demonstrations ranged from 69 percent at the 2017 Women's March to

31 percent at the People's Climate March, which built on the momentum of the active climate movement.

11. James M. Jasper and Jane D. Poulsen, "Recruiting Strangers and Friends: Moral Shocks and Social Networks in Animal Rights and Anti-Nuclear Protests," *Social Problems* 42, no. 4 (1995): 493–512, https://doi.org/10.2307/3097043; see also John D. McCarthy, "Pro-Life and Pro-Choice Mobilization: Infrastructure Deficits and New Technologies," in *Social Movements in an Organizational Society*, ed. M. N. Zald and John D. McCarthy (Piscataway, N. J.: Transaction, 1987), 48–66; Wayne A. Santoro and Marian Azab, "Arab American Protest in the Terror Decade: Macro- and Micro-Level Response to Post-9/11 Repression," *Social Problems* 62, no. 2 (May 2015): 219–40, https://doi.org/10.1093/socpro/spv004; Rachel G. McKane and Holly J. McCammon, "Why We March: The Role of Grievances, Threats, and Movement Organizational Resources in the 2017 Women's Marches," *Mobilization: An International Quarterly* 23, no. 4 (December 2018): 401–24, https://doi.org/10.17813/1086-671X-23-4-401.

12. For more discussion, see Dana R. Fisher, "Who Came Out in the Brutal Heat to the 'Families Belong Together' March? Here's Our Data," *Washington Post*, July 3, 2018, https://www.washingtonpost.com/news/monkey-cage/wp/2018/07/03/who-came-out-in-the-brutal-heat-to-the-families-belong-together-march-heres-our-data/.

13. Dana R. Fisher and Lorien Jasny, "Understanding Persistence in the Resistance," *Sociological Forum*, 2019, https://doi.org/10.31235/osf.io/y367j.

14. Kenneth T. Andrews, "How Protest Works," *New York Times*, October 21, 2017, https://www.nytimes.com/2017/10/21/opinion/sunday/how-protest-works.html; see also Zeynep Tufekci, *Twitter and Tear Gas: The Power and Fragility of Networked Protest* (New Haven, Conn.: Yale University Press, 2017).

15. Organizations were initially identified by a review of media coverage and discussions with groups working on the resistance in the streets. The list was then expanded to include groups that were mentioned repeatedly by respondents. All data were collected in accordance with the policies of the University of Maryland Institutional Review Board (IRB Protocol # 878998-3). Respondents are directly quoted when they gave formal approval to be named. For quotes that informants did not want directly attributed to them, a general affiliation is listed. Interviews

were recorded and then transcribed. For more details on sampling, research methods, and data analysis, see the appendix.

16. Karin Kamp, "The Indivisible Movement Is Fueling Resistance to Trump," *Salon*, February 15, 2017, https://www.salon.com/2017/02/15/how-the-indivisible-movement-is-fueling-resistance-to-trump_partner/; see also Charles Bethea, "The Crowdsourced Guide to Fighting Trump's Agenda," *The New Yorker*, December 16, 2016, https://www.newyorker.com/news/news-desk/the-crowd-sourced-guide-to-fighting-trumps-agenda; Megan E. Brooker, "Indivisible," in *The Resistance: The Dawn of the Anti-Trump Opposition Movement*, ed. David S. Meyer and Sidney Tarrow (New York: Oxford University Press, 2018), 162–84.

17. "Empower. 2017 Year in Review," *Indivisible*, https://www.indivisibleannualreport-2017.org/, accessed April 12, 2018.

18. Leah Greenberg, interview with author, October 9, 2018.

19. "Our Story," *Town Hall Project*, https://townhallproject.com/#ourStory, accessed April 13, 2018.

20. Map and details are available at https://docs.google.com/document/u/1/d/e/2PACX-1vSorDmXHT4DHFgp6KYH8d4NMT7WtJoP6AGKaRyNY2PHscZibC8oIWu4RUito2yoOB8-4c9oultd-6Ea/pub, accessed April 21, 2018.

21. "Missing Members," *Town Hall Project*, https://townhallproject.com/#missing-members, accessed November 24, 2018.

22. "The Town Hall Pledge," *Town Hall Project*, https://www.townhallpledge.com/, accessed November 24, 2018.

23. "About Swing Left," *Swing Left*, https://swingleft.org/about, accessed October 30, 2018.

24. Alex Roarty, "'Voting Isn't Enough.' Liberal Groups Band Together to Recruit Volunteers," *McClatchyDC*, July 17, 2018, https://www.mcclatchydc.com/news/politics-government/article214992200.html. See also the home page of The Last Weekend at https://thelastweekend.org/.

25. Bob Bland (aka Mari Lynn Foulger), interview with author, October 11, 2018. For more about Bland and her activism, see Katie Hintz-Zambrano, "Bob Bland of the Women's March on Raising Children in the Resistance, & Much More," *MOTHER*, September 1, 2017, http://www.mothermag.com/bob-bland-womens-march/.

26. Given the conflict among organizers of the national march and the sister marches, it is clear that I need to distinguish between the Women's March events, which have taken place around the United States organized by

a diversity of groups and the group that calls itself "Women's March." In the book, I refer to this group as the "National Women's March group." For an overview, see Marissa J. Lang, "What's in a Name? Women's March Groups Spar Over Who Owns the Name and the Movement," *Washington Post*, January 14, 2019, https://www.washingtonpost.com/local/whats-in-a-name -womens-march-groups-spar-over-who-owns-the-name-and-the-move ment/2019/01/14/354df744-15c3-11e9-b6ad-9cfd62dbb0a8_story.html.

27. For information on the school walkout, see "Enough: National School Walkout," *Action Network*, https://www.actionnetwork.org/event_campaigns /enough-national-school-walkout, accessed November 12, 2018; for more on the Hart Building protest, see Jason Newman, "Amy Schumer Arrested at Brett Kavanaugh Protest," *Rolling Stone*, October 4, 2018, https://www .rollingstone.com/politics/politics-news/amy-schumer-arrest-brett -kavanaugh-733221/.

28. For a full discussion, see Erica Chenoweth and Jeremy Pressman, "January's Women's March Brought Out More Than a Million People— and Many More Also Protested During the Month," *Washington Post*, February 26, 2018, https://www.washingtonpost.com/news/monkey-cage /wp/2018/02/26/januarys-womens-march-brought-out-more-than -a-million-people-and-many-more-also-protested-during-the -month/?utm_term=.a17c2c08cd2c.

29. For details, see Julia Felsenthal, "This Holiday Season, Give the Gift of Impeachment," *Vogue*, November 16, 2017, https://www.vogue.com /article/march-on-impeach-trump-vanessa-wruble; Farah Stockman, "One Year After Women's March, More Activism but Less Unity," *New York Times*, January 15, 2018, https://www.nytimes.com/2018/01/15 /us/womens-march-anniversary.html.

30. Vanessa Wruble, interview with author, February 9, 2018; see also Felsenthal, "This Holiday Season, Give the Gift of Impeachment."

31. Mustafa Santiago Ali, interview with author, January 8, 2018.

32. "A Short History of MoveOn," *MoveOn*, https://front.moveon.org /a-short-history/#.WtsɪvW4vzX4, accessed April 21, 2018; for more information on this group, see David Karpf, *The MoveOn Effect: The Unexpected Transformation of American Political Advocacy* (New York: Oxford University Press, 2012).

33. Victoria Kaplan, interview with author, February 20, 2018; for informa- tion on the Women's March partners, see https://www.womensmarch .com/partners, accessed April 23, 2018 (no longer available; Wikipedia has

a version at https://en.wikipedia.org/wiki/2017_Women%27s_March;
for more on the family separations protest, see Justin Krebs, "In 750
Cities, We Marched: Families Belong Together," *MoveOn*, https://front.
moveon.org/in-750-cities-we-marched-families-belong-together/;
see also Fisher, "Who Came Out in the Brutal Heat to the 'Families
Belong Together' March?"

34. Lucy Westcott, "Thousands of Lawyers Descend on U.S. Airports to
Fight Trump's Immigrant Ban," *Newsweek*, January 29, 2017, http://
www.newsweek.com/lawyers-volunteer-us-airports-trump-ban-549830;
for more details, see Michael C. Dorf and Michael S. Chu, "Lawyers
as Activists," in *The Resistance: The Dawn of the Anti-Trump Opposition
Movement*, ed. David S. Meyer and Sidney Tarrow (New York: Oxford
University Press, 2018), 127–42. For a useful timeline, see "Timeline of
the Muslim Ban," *ACLU Washington*, https://www.aclu-wa.org/pages
/timeline-muslim-ban, accessed April 23, 2018.

35. Faiz Shakir, "How the ACLU Plans to Engage in the 2018 Midterm Elections," *American Civil Liberties Union*, January 11, 2018, https://www.aclu
.org/blog/mobilization/how-aclu-plans-engage-2018-midterm-elections.

36. Victoria Kaplan, interview with author, October 12, 2018.

37. Phil Aroneanu, interview with author, October 30, 2018.

38. Doug McAdam and Sidney Tarrow, "Ballots and Barricades: On the
Reciprocal Relationship Between Elections and Social Movements,"
Perspectives on Politics 8, no. 2 (June 2010): 529–42, https://doi.org/10.1017
/S1537592710001234; see also Doug McAdam, Sidney Tarrow, and Charles
Tilly, *Dynamics of Contention* (New York: Cambridge University Press,
2001); Dana R. Fisher, "Youth Political Participation: Bridging Activism
and Electoral Politics," *Annual Review of Sociology* 38 (2012): 119–37;
Michael T. Heaney and Fabio Rojas, *Party in the Street: The Antiwar
Movement and the Democratic Party After 9/11* (New York: Cambridge
University Press, 2015).

39. Edward T. Walker, "Privatizing Participation: Civic Change and the
Organizational Dynamics of Grassroots Lobbying Firms," *American
Sociological Review* 74, no. 1 (2009): 83–105; Theda Skocpol, *Dimin-
ished Democracy: From Membership to Management in American Civic
Life* (Norman: University of Oklahoma Press, 2013); see also Verba,
Schlozman, and Brady, *Voice and Equality*; Robert D. Putnam, *Bowling
Alone: The Collapse and Revival of American Community* (New York:
Touchstone Books, Simon & Schuster, 2000).

40. For a full discussion, see Dana R. Fisher, *Activism, Inc.: How the Outsourcing of Grassroots Campaigns Is Strangling Progressive Politics in America* (Stanford, Calif.: Stanford University Press, 2006), especially chap. 5.

41. Dohl interview with author, January 16, 2018.

42. Anson Kaye, "50-State Strategy for Dems? How About 15 Instead?", *The Hill*, March 2, 2017, http://thehill.com/blogs/pundits-blog/national -party-news/321998-50-state-strategy-for-dems-how-about-15-instead; Robert Kuttner, "Q&A: A New 50-State Strategy," *American Prospect*, January 17, 2017, http://prospect.org/article/qa-new-50-state-strategy; Laura Barrón-López, "Some Democrats Aren't Buying the DNC's New 50-State Strategy," *Washington Examiner*, February 4, 2018, https://www .washingtonexaminer.com/some-democrats-arent-buying-the-dncs -new-50-state-strategy. For an overview, see "The 50-State Strategy," *DNC*, https://democrats.org/the-50-state-strategy/, accessed April 20, 2018.

43. Mustafa Ali Santiago, interview with author, January 8, 2018; Vanessa Wruble, interview with author, October 24, 2018.

44. John Sides, "How Democrats Are Dominating Special Elections— in One Graph," *Washington Post*, December 13, 2017, https://www .washingtonpost.com/news/monkey-cage/wp/2017/12/13/how -democrats-are-dominating-special-elections-in-one-graph/?utm _term=.c9doc659442d; Joan Walsh, "Here's Why Democrats Won Big in Virginia," *The Nation*, November 8, 2017, https://www.thenation.com /article/heres-why-democrats-won-big-in-virginia/; for an analysis of turnout for special elections, see Nate Silver, "Another Special Election, Another Really Bad Sign for the GOP," *FiveThirtyEight*, April 25, 2018, https://fivethirtyeight.com/features/arizona-8-special-election-result/.

45. Phil Aroneanu, interview with author, January 19, 2018.

46. Ethan Todras-Whitehill, interview with author, January 19, 2018. Swing Left and Flippable merged in May 2019.

47. See Alana Abramson, "Republicans Are Investing Campaign Cash in the Party. Democrats Are Investing in Candidates," *Fortune*, February 6, 2018, http://fortune.com/2018/02/06/campaign-fundraising-2018-election -democrats-republicans/; Tim Dickinson, "How Progressive Activists Are Leading the Trump Resistance," *Rolling Stone*, August 24, 2017, http://www.rollingstone.com/politics/features/how-progressive -activists-are-leading-the-trump-resistance-w499221; Branco Marcetic, "Here's Who the Democrats Want You to Vote for This November,"

The Jacobin Magazine, April 2018, http://jacobinmag.com/2018/04/democratic-party-red-to-blue-list-candidates.

48. See James Arkin and Scott Bland, "Top Democrat Crowley Loses in Shocker," *Politico*, June 26, 2018, https://politi.co/2tFPfHV; John Nichols, "Ayanna Pressley Wins a Fight for the Soul of the Democratic Party," *The Nation*, September 4, 2018, https://www.thenation.com/article/ayanna-pressley-wins-a-fight-for-the-soul-of-the-democratic-party/.

49. Lawrence Douglas, "The Democratic Party Is Now Publicly Attacking Progressive Candidates," *The Guardian*, February 26, 2018, https://www.theguardian.com/commentisfree/2018/feb/26/democratic-party-laura-moser-texas.

50. For a discussion of recent efforts in primaries, see Aaron Blake, "Why Steve Bannon's Threat to Primary Almost Every GOP Senator Should Frighten Republicans," *Washington Post*, October 10, 2017, https://www.washingtonpost.com/news/the-fix/wp/2017/10/10/why-steve-bannons-targeting-of-incumbent-senators-is-a-serious-threat-to-the-gop/; for examples of resistance groups supporting primary candidates in Illinois and California, see David Weigel and Michael Scherer, "The 2018 Midterms Are Fast Approaching. First Up: Primary Fights for Both Parties' Future," *Washington Post*, January 6, 2018, https://www.washingtonpost.com/powerpost/the-2018-midterms-are-fast-approaching-first-up-primary-fights-for-both-parties-future/2018/01/06/3b3d20fe-f1b0-11e7-b3bf-ab90a706e175_story.html.

51. Leah Greenberg, interview with author, October 9, 2018.

52. Fisher, *Activism, Inc.*, 96; for a more recent discussion, see Lara Putnam and Theda Skocpol, "Middle America Reboots Democracy," *Democracy Journal*, February 20, 2018, https://democracyjournal.org/arguments/middle-america-reboots-democracy/.

53. Catherine Vaughan, interview with author, January 26, 2018.

54. Off-the-record interview with resistance group leader, January 2018.

55. Phil Aroneanu, interview with author, October 10, 2018; Victoria Kaplan, interview with author, October 12, 2018; Sarah Dohl, interview with author, January 16, 2018.

56. See, for example, Carmen Sirianni and Lewis Friedland, *Civic Innovation in America: Community Empowerment, Public Policy, and the Movement for Civic Renewal* (Berkeley: University of California Press, 2001); Harry Chatten Boyte, *Everyday Politics: Reconnecting Citizens and Public Life*

(Philadelphia: University of Pennsylvania Press, 2004); Carmen Sirianni, *Varieties of Civic Innovation: Deliberative, Collaborative, Network, and Narrative Approaches* (Nashville, Tenn.: Vanderbilt University Press, 2014); Dana R. Fisher, Erika S. Svendsen, and James J. Connolly, *Urban Environmental Stewardship and Civic Engagement* (New York: Routledge, 2015), https://doi.org/10.4324/9781315857589; William Yagatich, Anya M. Galli Robertson, and Dana R. Fisher, "How Local Environmental Stewardship Diversifies Democracy," *Local Environment* 23, no. 4 (April 2018): 431–47, https://doi.org/10.1080/13549839.2018.1428187.

57. Kuttner, "Q&A: A New 50-State Strategy"; for discussion of organizing through the Obama campaign, see Ari Melber, "Year One of Organizing for America: The Permanent Field Campaign in a Digital Age," *techPresident Special Report.* January 14, 2010, 74, www.techpresident.com/ofayear1; see also Micah L. Sifry, "Obama's Lost Army," *The New Republic*, February 9, 2017, https://newrepublic.com/article/140245/obamas-lost-army-inside-fall-grassroots-machine.

58. Victoria Kaplan, interview with author, October 12, 2018; off-the-record interview with resistance group leader, October 2018. The lack of a clear definition was not particularly surprising given that I was only able to find written examples rather than formal definitions, see Becky Bond and Zack Exley, *Rules for Revolutionaries: How Big Organizing Can Change Everything* (White River Junction, Vt.: Chelsea Green, 2016).

59. For details, see Karpf, *The MoveOn Effect.*

60. Leah Greenberg, interview with author, October 9, 2018; Vanessa Wruble, interview with author, October 24, 2018. For a discussion of how this Maoist saying has been used in progressive politics, see Bond and Exley, *Rules for Revolutionaries*, chap. 6.

61. See Kenneth Andrews and Bob Edwards, "The Organizational Structure of Local Environmentalism," *Mobilization: An International Quarterly* 10, no. 2 (June 2005): 213–34, https://doi.org/10.17813/maiq.10.2.028028u600744073; Dana R. Fisher, Lindsay K. Campbell, and Erika S. Svendsen, "The Organisational Structure of Urban Environmental Stewardship," *Environmental Politics* 21, no. 1 (2012): 26–48; for more on the federated model, see Skocpol, *Diminished Democracy;* Theda Skocpol, Marshall Ganz, and Ziad Munson, "A Nation of Organizers: The Institutional Origins of Civic Voluntarism in the United States," *The American Political Science Review* 94, no. 3 (2000): 527–46, https://doi.org/10.2307/2585829.

62. Elisabeth S. Clemens, *The People's Lobby: Organizational Innovation and the Rise of Interest Group Politics in the United States, 1890–1925* (Chicago: University of Chicago Press, 1997).

63. Phil Aroneanu, interview with author, January 19, 2018.

64. Bond and Exley, *Rules for Revolutionaries.*

65. For an overview, see Caroline W. Lee, "Participatory Practices in Organizations," *Sociology Compass* 9, no. 4 (April 2015): 272–88, https://doi.org/10.1111/soc4.12252; but see Nina Eliasoph, "Top-Down Civic Projects Are Not Grassroots Associations: How the Differences Matter in Everyday Life," *VOLUNTAS: International Journal of Voluntary and Nonprofit Organizations* 20, no. 3 (September 2009): 291–308, https://doi.org/10.1007/s11266-009-9087-y.

66. Bob Bland, interview with author, October 11, 2018; Leah Greenberg, interview with author, October 10, 2018.

67. Leah Greenberg, interview with author, October 9, 2018; "Leader's Corner," *Indivisible,* https://indivisible.org/leaders-corner, accessed December 8, 2018.

68. Phil Aroneanu, interview with author, October 10, 2018.

69. "About Swing Left," *Swing Left,* https://swingleft.org/about, accessed November 15, 2018.

70. Evan Halper, "Dramatic Improvements in Campaign Technology Reshaped the Midterm Election: The Presidential Race Awaits," *LA Times,* December 1, 2018, https://www.latimes.com/politics/la-na-pol-campaign-tech-20181129-story.html.

71. Victoria Kaplan, interview with author, October 12, 2018; Phil Aroneanu, interview with author, October 10, 2018.

72. Phil Aroneanu, interview with author, October 10, 2018.

73. Victoria Kaplan, interview with author, October 12, 2018; see also "Join a Wave: Resist & Win. Voter Contact Day of Action," *MoveOn,* https://act.moveon.org/event/waves_attend/search/, accessed December 9, 2018.

74. "Why We Marched. #MarchForOurLives," *Hip Hop Caucus,* March 29, 2018, http://hiphopcaucus.org/marchforourlives/.

75. Ethan Todras-Whitehill, interview with author, January 19, 2018.

76. For a history of this type of instrumental politics, see Fisher, *Activism, Inc.*

77. See Farah Stockman, "Women's March Roiled by Accusations of Anti-Semitism," *New York Times,* December 24, 2018, https://www.nytimes.com/2018/12/23/us/womens-march-anti-semitism.html; Vanessa Wruble, interview with author, February 9, 2018.

78. For an overview, see Suzanne Staggenborg, "The Consequences of Professionalization and Formalization in the Pro-Choice Movement," *American Sociological Review* 53, no. 4 (1988): 585–605, https://doi.org /10.2307/2095851.

79. Nella Van Dyke and Holly J. McCammon, *Strategic Alliances: Coalition Building and Social Movements* (Minneapolis: University of Minnesota Press, 2010).

4. RESISTANCE IN THE DISTRICTS

1. March for Science S|GNS Summit 2018 Conference Guide, https:// www.marchforscience.com/summit-about.

2. Research America, Vote for Science, https://www.researchamerica.org /news-events/newsletter/vote-science, accessed May 30, 2019.

3. Doug McAdam and Karina Kloos, *Deeply Divided: Racial Politics and Social Movements in Postwar America* (New York: Oxford University Press, 2014), 10.

4. Michael T. Heaney and Fabio Rojas, *Party in the Street: The Antiwar Movement and the Democratic Party After 9/11* (New York: Cambridge University Press, 2015); McAdam and Kloos, *Deeply Divided*; see also Doug McAdam and Sidney Tarrow, "Ballots and Barricades: On the Reciprocal Relationship Between Elections and Social Movements," *Perspectives on Politics* 8, no. 2 (June 2010): 529–42, https://doi.org/10.1017/S1537592710001234.

5. See also Dana R. Fisher, Lorien Jasny, and Dawn M. Dow, "Why Are We Here? Patterns of Intersectional Motivations Across the Resistance," *Mobilization: An International Quarterly* 23, no. 4 (December 2018): 451–68.

6. For details, see Dana R. Fisher, "Climate of Resistance: How the Climate Movement Connects to the Resistance," in *The Resistance: The Dawn of the Anti-Trump Opposition Movement*, ed. David S. Meyer and Sidney Tarrow (New York: Oxford University Press, 2018), chap. 5.

7. For example, see Perry Stein and Sandhya Somashekhar, "It Started with a Retiree. Now the Women's March Could Be the Biggest Inauguration Demonstration," *Washington Post*, January 3, 2017, https://www .washingtonpost.com/national/it-started-with-a-grandmother-in-hawaii -now-the-womens-march-on-washington-is-poised-to-be-the-biggest -inauguration-demonstration/2017/01/03/8af61686-c6e2-11e6-bf4b-2c06 4d32a4bf_story.html; Ben Guarino, "The March for Science Began with

This Person's 'Throwaway Line' on Reddit," *Washington Post*, April 21, 2017, https://www.washingtonpost.com/news/speaking-of-science/wp/2017/04/21/the-march-for-science-began-with-this-persons-throwaway-line-on-reddit/.

8. Alan Schussman and Sarah Anne Soule, "Process and Protest: Accounting for Individual Protest Participation," *Social Forces* 84, no. 2 (2005): 1092, https://doi.org/10.1353/sof.2006.0034.

9. For details, see Dana R. Fisher, Kevin Stanley, David Berman, and Gina Neff, "How Do Organizations Matter? Mobilization and Support for Participants at Five Globalization Protests," *Social Problems* 52, no. 1 (February 2005): 102–21, https://doi.org/10.1525/sp.2005.52.1.102.

10. Bert Klandermans, Jacquelien van Stekelenburg, Marie-Louise Damen, Dunya van Troost, and Anouk van Leeuwen, "Mobilization Without Organization: The Case of Unaffiliated Demonstrators," *European Sociological Review* 30, no. 6 (2014): 707–716, doi:, https://doi.org/10.1093/esr/jcu068.

11. Dana R. Fisher, "On Social Networks and Social Protest: Understanding the Role of Organizational and Personal Ties in Large-Scale Protest Events," in *Research in Social Movements, Conflicts and Change*, Vol. 30, ed. Patrick G. Coy (Bingley, U.K.: Emerald Group, 2010), 115–40, https://doi.org/10.1108/S0163-786X(2010)0000030007.

12. David Karpf, *The MoveOn Effect: The Unexpected Transformation of American Political Advocacy* (New York: Oxford University Press, 2012), 24, xii–xiii.

13. See, especially, Hahrie Han, *How Organizations Develop Activists: Civic Associations and Leadership in the 21st Century* (New York: Oxford University Press, 2014); Kenneth T. Andrews, "How Protest Works," *New York Times*, October 21, 2017, https://www.nytimes.com/2017/10/21/opinion/sunday/how-protest-works.html.

14. Differences in these surveys may be due, in part, to differences in the response rate and who responded to each wave of the survey (see appendix for details).

15. For a discussion, see Theda Skocpol, *Diminished Democracy: From Membership to Management in American Civic Life* (Norman: University of Oklahoma Press, 2013).

16. Neal Caren, Raj Andrew Ghoshal, and Vanesa Ribas, "A Social Movement Generation: Cohort and Period Trends in Protest Attendance and

Petition Signing," *American Sociological Review* 76, no. 1 (February 2011): 147, https://doi.org/10.1177/0003122410395369.

17. Erica Chenoweth and Jeremy Pressman, "This Is What We Learned by Counting the Women's Marches," *Washington Post*, February 7, 2017, https://www.washingtonpost.com/news/monkey-cage/wp/2017/02/07/this-is-what-we-learned-by-counting-the-womens-marches/.

18. William Wan, "Postcards from the Left: Resistance Groups Take Aim at Trump, One Letter at a Time," *Washington Post*, November 2, 2018, https://www.washingtonpost.com/national/postcards-from-the-left-resistance-groups-take-aim-at-trump-one-letter-at-a-time/2018/11/02/699df7e0-c1ba-11e8-a1fo-a4051b6ad114_story.html?utm_term=.13ee49fb664c.

19. Lara Putnam and Theda Skocpol, "Women Are Rebuilding the Democratic Party from the Ground Up," *The New Republic*, August 21, 2018, https://newrepublic.com/article/150462/women-rebuilding-democratic-party-ground.

20. "Flip the USA Blue: Send Letters to Unlikely Voters," *Vote Forward*, https://votefwd.org/, accessed December 23, 2018.

21. See Skocpol, *Diminished Democracy*; Theda Skocpol, Marshall Ganz, and Ziad Munson, "A Nation of Organizers: The Institutional Origins of Civic Voluntarism in the United States," *The American Political Science Review* 94, no. 3 (2000): 527–46, https://doi.org/10.2307/2585829; see also Jeffrey M. Berry and Clyde Wilcox, *Interest Group Society*, 5th ed. (New York: Routledge, 2008).

22. For a full discussion, see Dana R. Fisher, Dawn M. Dow, and Rashawn Ray, "Intersectionality Takes It to the Streets: Mobilizing Across Diverse Interests for the Women's March," *Science Advances* 3, no. 9 (September 2017): eaao1390, https://doi.org/10.1126/sciadv.aao1390; Fisher, Jasny, and Dow, "Why Are We Here? Patterns of Intersectional Motivations Across the Resistance."

23. A federal judge in Texas ruled the Affordable Care Act unconstitutional under new federal tax law after the midterm elections in December 2018. For a discussion, see Amy Goldstein, "Federal Judge in Texas Rules Entire Obama Health-Care Law Is Unconstitutional," *Washington Post*, December 14, 2018, https://www.washingtonpost.com/national/health-science/federal-judge-in-texas-rules-obama-health-care-law-unconstitutional/2018/12/14/9e8bb5a2-fd63-11e8-862a-b6a6f3ce8199_story.html.

24. Pew Research Center, "Voter Enthusiasm at Record High in Nation-alized Midterm Environment," September 26, 2018, http://www.people-press.org/2018/09/26/voter-enthusiasm-at-record-high-in-nationalized-midterm-environment/.

25. For a full discussion of priming effects, see Daniel C. Molden, ed., *Understanding Priming Effects in Social Psychology* (New York: Guilford Press, 2014).

26. Although only six categories align, the Pew survey's category "treatment of ethnic and racial minorities" overlapped with both my civil rights and racial justice categories.

27. Citizens United v. Federal Election Comm'n 558 U.S. 310 (2010).

28. Brady Dennis and Julliet Eilpern, "Scott Pruitt Steps Down as EPA Head After Ethics, Management Scandals," *Washington Post*, July 7, 2018, https://www.washingtonpost.com/national/health-science/trump-epa-head-steps-down-after-wave-of-ethics-management-scandals/2018/07/05/39f4251a-6813-11e8-bea7-c8eb28bc52b1_story.html.

29. For a full discussion, see Robert B. McKinstry Jr., "What Really Happened? Implications of President Trump's Announcement on U.S. Withdrawal from the Paris Agreement and the Law of Unintended Consequences," *National Law Review*, September 4, 2017, https://www.natlawreview.com/article/what-really-happened-implications-president-trump-s-announcement-us-withdrawal-paris.

30. The focus on more progressive solutions in the second wave of the follow-up survey may be due, in part, to differences in those who partic-ipated in this survey (for discussion, see the appendix).

31. Paul chose not to answer the question about race.

32. Seymour Martin Lipset and Gary Wolfe Marks, *It Didn't Happen Here: Why Socialism Failed in the United States* (New York: Norton, 2001); see also Louis Hartz, *The Liberal Tradition in America: An Interpreta-tion of American Political Thought Since the Revolution* (Boston, Mass.: Houghton Mifflin Harcourt, 1955); Kim Voss, *The Making of American Exceptionalism: The Knights of Labor and Class Formation in the Nineteenth Century* (Ithaca, N.Y.: Cornell University Press, 1994).

5. LOOKING BACK WHILE MARCHING FORWARD

1. Marissa J. Lang, "The Women's March in Year 3: Can the Movement Overcome a Year of Controversy and Division?", *Washington Post*,

January 18, 2019, https://www.washingtonpost.com/local/the-womens
-march-in-year-3-can-the-movement-overcome-a-year-of-controversy
-and-division/2019/01/17/0eb23740-18c9-11e9-8813-cb9dec761e73_story
.html.

2. National turnout was estimated at between 665,324-735,978 people. It
was smaller, in part due to the weather around the country. For details,
see Erica Chenoweth and Jeremy Pressman. "The 2019 Women's March
Was Bigger than You Think." *Washington Post*, February 1, 2019, https://
www.washingtonpost.com/news/monkey-cage/wp/2019/02/01/the-2019
-womens-march-was-bigger-than-you-think/?utm_term=.f42a681cf988/.

3. S. Erdem Aytac and Susan Stokes, "Americans Just Set a Turnout Record
for the Midterms, Voting at the Highest Rate Since 1914. This Explains
Why," *Washington Post*, January 20, 2018, https://www.washingtonpost
.com/news/monkey-cage/wp/2018/11/20/americans-just-set-a-turnout
-record-for-the-midterms-voting-at-the-highest-rate-since-1914-this
-explains-why/.

4. August H. Nimtz, "The Graveyard of Progressive Social Movements,"
MR Online (blog), May 9, 2017, https://mronline.org/2017/05/09/the
-graveyard-of-progressive-social-movements/.

5. For details, see Michael T. Heaney and Fabio Rojas, *Party in the Street:
The Antiwar Movement and the Democratic Party After 9/11* (New York:
Cambridge University Press, 2015); Micah L. Sifry, "Obama's Lost
Army," *The New Republic*, February 9, 2017, https://newrepublic.com
/article/140245/obamas-lost-army-inside-fall-grassroots-machine.

6. For details, see Katie Hogan, "What OFA Has Accomplished, and
the Fight Ahead," https://medium.com/allontheline/what-ofa-has
-accomplished-and-the-fight-ahead-2c3190060f8c, accessed January 17,
2019.

7. Elizabeth McKenna, Hahrie Han, and Jeremy Bird, *Groundbreakers: How Obama's 2.2 Million Volunteers Transformed Campaigning in
America* (New York: Oxford University Press, 2015), 171. See also Han,
Hahrie, and Lara Putnam. "The Best Way for Democrats to Win in
2020? By Ignoring the Candidates for Now." *Washington Post*, April 29,
2019, https://www.washingtonpost.com/outlook/2019/04/29/best-way
-democrats-win-by-ignoring-candidates-now/.

8. Across all of the marches, the overwhelming majority of participants
are American citizens. To download estimates of the size of the protests
against the Trump administration by month, see the Crowd Counting

Consortium, "View/Download the Data," https://sites.google.com/view
/crowdcountingconsortium/view-download-the-data?authuser=0,
accessed January 16, 2019.

9. Lara Putnam and Theda Skocpol, "Women Are Rebuilding the Democratic Party from the Ground Up," *The New Republic*, August 21, 2018,
https://newrepublic.com/article/150462/women-rebuilding-demo
cratic-party-ground; see also Dana R Fisher, "This Year's Women's
Marchers Weren't Focused on the Leadership Controversy. They Were
All About Local and National Political Organizing," *Washington Post*,
January 22, 2019, https://www.washingtonpost.com/news/monkey-cage
/wp/2019/01/22/this-years-womens-marchers-werent-focused-on
-the-leadership-controversy-they-were-all-about-local-and-national
-political-organizing/.

10. For 2018 turnout data, see Alec Tyson, "The 2018 Midterm Vote:
Divisions by Race, Gender, and Education," *Pew Research Center*,
November 8, 2018, http://www.pewresearch.org/fact-tank/2018/11/08
/the-2018-midterm-vote-divisions-by-race-gender-education/; see also
Putnam and Skocpol, "Women Are Rebuilding the Democratic Party
From the Ground Up"; Putnam and Skocpol, "Middle America Reboots
Democracy."

11. Adapted from Doug McAdam and Sidney Tarrow, "Ballots and
Barricades: On the Reciprocal Relationship Between Elections and
Social Movements," *Perspectives on Politics* 8, no. 2 (June 2010): 529–42,
https://doi.org/10.1017/S1537592710001234.

12. Francesca Polletta and James M. Jasper, "Collective Identity and Social
Movements," *Annual Review of Sociology* 27, no. 1 (2001): 283–305,
https://doi.org/10.1146/annurev.soc.27.1.283.

13. Doug McAdam and Karina Kloos, *Deeply Divided: Racial Politics and
Social Movements in Postwar America* (New York: Oxford University
Press, 2014), 10. This distinction is discussed in detail in Doug McAdam,
Sidney Tarrow, and Charles Tilly, *The Dynamics of Contention* (New York:
Cambridge University Press, 2001), in which they disaggregate what they
call "contained" and "transgressive" forms of contention.

14. It was well known that the path to a Democratic majority in the Senate
in 2018 was unlikely. See Nathaniel Rakich, "Democrats' Horrible 2018
Senate Map Couldn't Have Come at a Better Time," *FiveThirtyEight*,
May 1, 2018, https://fivethirtyeight.com/features/democrats-horrible-2018
-senate-map-couldnt-have-come-at-a-better-time/.

15. Heaney and Rojas, *Party in the Street*, 230, 229.
16. See discussion in David Karpf, *The MoveOn Effect: The Unexpected Transformation of American Political Advocacy* (New York: Oxford University Press, 2012).
17. Dana R. Fisher, *Activism, Inc.: How the Outsourcing of Grassroots Campaigns Is Strangling Progressive Politics in America* (Stanford, Calif.: Stanford University Press, 2006).
18. Jennifer Earl and Katrina Kimport, *Digitally Enabled Social Change: Activism in the Internet Age* (Cambridge, Mass.: MIT Press, 2013).
19. These findings are consistent with arguments made by David Karpf, *Analytic Activism: Digital Listening and the New Political Strategy* (New York: Oxford University Press, 2016).
20. Rachel G. McKane and Holly J. McCammon, "Why We March: The Role of Grievances, Threats, and Movement Organizational Resources in the 2017 Women's Marches," *Mobilization: An International Quarterly* 23, no. 4 (December 2018): 419, https://doi.org/10.17813/1086-671X-23-4-401.
21. Jeffrey M. Berry and Sarah Sobieraj, *The Outrage Industry: Political Opinion Media and the New Incivility* (New York: Oxford University Press, 2014).
22. See "Rapid-Response Events," *MoveOn*, https://act.moveon.org/event /mueller-firing-rapid-response-events/search/, accessed January 14, 2019; see also T. J. Ortenzi, "'Protect Mueller': Protesters Across U.S. Decry President's Dismissal of Sessions as Attorney General," *Washington Post*, November 8, 2018, https://www.washingtonpost.com/nation/2018/11/09 /no-one-is-above-law-protesters-across-us-say-trump-threatens-muellers -investigation-by-replacing-sessions/. For crowd estimates, see Crowd Counting Consortium, "Crowd Estimates November 2018," https://docs .google.com/spreadsheets/d/1tmUwI_SnhW5qv6JAxCqRuof6e YmhUf6V-wtUdi5AXTQ/edit#gid=995673643, accessed November 24, 2018.
23. Leah Greenberg, email correspondence with author, January 17, 2019.
24. Eliza Barclay, "Photos: Kids in 123 Countries Went on Strike to Protect the Climate," *Vox*, March 15, 2019, https://www.vox.com/energy-and -environment/2019/3/15/18267156/youth-climate-strike-march-15 -photos.
25. Nolan D. McCaskill and John Bresnahan, "CBC Votes No Confidence in Democratic Chair Perez," *Politico*, November 14, 2018, https://politi .co/2B8PAIl.

26. Alex Thompson, "DNC Chair Tom Perez Goes to War with State Parties," *Politico*, December 16, 2018, https://politi.co/2Bsl7Ui; Alex Thompson, "Democrats Seek Cease-Fire in Voter Data Wars," *Politico*, December 19, 2018, https://politi.co/2BwjkoI.

27. Rachel Bade and Heather Caygle, "Exasperated Democrats Try to Rein in Ocasio-Cortez," *Politico*, January 11, 2019, https://www.politico.com /story/2019/01/11/alexandria-ocasio-cortez-democrats-establisment -1093728.

28. For an overview of the controversies, see Marissa J. Lang, "What's in a Name? Women's March Groups Spar over Who Owns the Name and the Movement," *Washington Post*, January 14, 2019, https:// www.washingtonpost.com/local/whats-in-a-name-womens-march -groups-spar-over-who-owns-the-name-and-the-movement/2019 /01/14/354df744-15c3-11e9-b6ad-9cfd62dbb0a8_story.html.

29. See, for example, Elisabeth S. Clemens, *The People's Lobby: Organizational Innovation and the Rise of Interest Group Politics in the United States, 1890–1925* (Chicago: University of Chicago Press, 1997); Theda Skocpol, Marshall Ganz, and Ziad Munson, "A Nation of Organizers: The Institutional Origins of Civic Voluntarism in the United States," *American Political Science Review* 94, no. 3 (2000): 527–46, https://doi .org/10.2307/2585829; Theda Skocpol, *Diminished Democracy: From Membership to Management in American Civic Life* (Norman: University of Oklahoma Press, 2013).

30. Tara McGowan, "Trump Is Already Winning 2020," *The Hill*, February 7, 2019, https://thehill.com/opinion/campaign/428937-trump-is-already -winning-2020.

31. Toluse Olorunnipa and Josh Dawsey, "Trump's Massive Reelection Campaign Has 2016 Themes—And a 2020 Infrastructure," *Washington Post*, March 10, 2019, https://www.washingtonpost.com/politics/trumps -massive-reelection-campaign-has-2016-themes--and-a-2020 -infrastructure/2019/03/10/5f44109c-4124-11e9-a0d3-1210e58a94cf_story .html?utm_term=.b9690226e980.

32. For an overview, see Boris Heersink, "No, the DNC Didn't 'Rig' the Democratic Primary for Hillary Clinton," *Washington Post*, November 4, 2017, https://www.washingtonpost.com/news/monkey-cage/wp/2017/11/04 /no-the-dnc-didnt-rig-the-democratic-primary-for-hillary-clinton/.

33. On environmental issues, see Steven Rattner, "Yes, We Need a Green New Deal. Just Not the One Alexandria Ocasio-Cortez Is Offering,"

New York Times, March 21, 2019, https://www.nytimes.com/2019/03/20 /opinion/green-new-deal-carbon-taxes.html; David Roberts, "There's Now an Official Green New Deal. Here's What's in It," *Vox*, February 7, 2019, https://www.vox.com/energy-and-environment/2019/2/7/18211709 /green-new-deal-resolution-alexandria-ocasio-cortez-markey. On the reform of political power, see Ella Nilsen, "House Democrats Just Passed a Slate of Significant Reforms to Get Money Out of Politics," *Vox*, March 8, 2019, https://www.vox.com/2019/3/8/18253609/hr-1-pelosi-house -democrats-anti-corruption-mcconnell.

34. Kate Ackley, "'No PAC Money' Pledges Leave Corporations in a Partisan Bind," *Roll Call*, March 21, 2019, https://www.rollcall.com /news/congress/leaders-pacs-may-shift-gears; James Hohmann, "The Daily 202: Bernie Sanders Sounds Less 'Radical' Than He Did in 2016 Because Democrats Have Moved His Way," *Washington Post*, March 11, 2019, https://www.washingtonpost.com/news/powerpost/paloma/daily -202/2019/03/11/daily-202-bernie-sanders-sounds-less-radical-than -he-did-in-2016-because-democrats-have-moved-his-way/5c856a8e1b 326b2d177d6040/.

METHODOLOGICAL APPENDIX

1. Stefaan Walgrave and Joris Verhulst, "Selection and Response Bias in Protest Surveys," *Mobilization: An International Quarterly* 16, no. 2 (June 2011): 203–22, doi: https://doi.org/10.17813/maiq.16.2.j475m8627u4u8177; Stefaan Walgrave, Ruud Wouters, and Pauline Ketelaars, "Response Problems in the Protest Survey Design: Evidence from Fifty-One Protest Events in Seven Countries," *Mobilization: An International Quarterly* 21, no. 1 (March 2016): 83–104, doi: https://doi.org/10.17813/108 6/671X-21-1-83.

2. Isabelle Bédoyan, Peter Aelst, and Stefaan Walgrave, "Limitations and Possibilities of Transnational Mobilization: The Case of EU Summit Protesters in Brussels, 2001," *Mobilization: An International Quarterly* 9, no. 1 (February 2004): 39–54, doi: https://doi.org/10.17813/maiq.9.1 .d599r28j75356jp1; Dana R. Fisher, Kevin Stanley, David Berman, and Gina Neff, "How Do Organizations Matter? Mobilization and Support for Participants at Five Globalization Protests," *Social Problems* 52, no. 1 (February 2005): 102–21, doi: https://doi.org/10.1525/sp.2005.52.1.102; Michael T. Heaney and Fabio Rojas, *Party in the Street: The Antiwar*

Movement and the Democratic Party After 9/11 (New York: Cambridge University Press, 2015).

3. Walgrave and Verhulst, "Selection and Response Bias in Protest Surveys"; Walgrave, Wouters, and Ketelaars, "Response Problems in the Protest Survey Design."

4. Survey instruments are posted at https://osf.io/fdbzk/.

5. Very few people offered phone numbers without email addresses.

6. As a member of these groups, I received numerous emails after the midterm elections.

7. For a discussion on response rates, see Dana R. Fisher, "Taking Cover Beneath the Anti-Bush Umbrella: Cycles of Protest and Movement -to-Movement Transmission in an Era of Repressive Politics," *Research in Political Sociology* 15 (2006): 27–56, at n20.

8. Statistical significance is assessed at the .005 level.

9. John Lofland and Lyn H. Lofland, *Analyzing Social Settings: A Guide to Qualitative Observation and Analysis* (Belmont, Calif.: Wadsworth, 1995), 5.

INDEX

Page numbers in *italics* indicate figures or tables.